Aromas and Flavors

Aromas and Flavors

OF PAST AND PRESENT

Alice B. Toklas

WITH INTRODUCTION

AND COMMENTS

BY POPPY CANNON

THE LYONS PRESS

Library of Congress Cataloging–in–Publication Data
Toklas, Alice B.
    Aromas and flavors of past and present / Alice B.
Toklas with introduction and comments by Poppy
Cannon.
        p.   cm.   — (The cook's classic library)
    Originally published: New York: Harper & Brothers,
1958.
    ISBN 1-55821-633-2
    1. Cookery, French. I. Title. II. Series.
TX719.T62 1998
641.5944—dc21   97-31777
                                                      CIP

CONTENTS

INTRODUCTION

BY POPPY CANNON

When all the world became aware through Gertrude Stein that a rose is a rose is a rose is a rose, this was the culmination of a many-sided artistic revolution that began in Paris more than fifty years ago. Gertrude Stein was one of a group of evolutionaries—a group that included, to mention just a few, Picasso, Matisse and Juan Gris. These and many others through the years found a kind of home place in the Left Bank ménage shared by Gertrude Stein and her friend Alice B. Toklas.

Not only in the book called *The Autobiography of Alice B. Toklas* by Gertrude Stein but also in *The Alice B. Toklas Cook Book,* published in 1954, the rich years are described in which "Miss Stein wrote and talked, Miss Toklas cooked and talked."

The cooking was in its way as important and significant as all the other artistic activities that flourished in that burgeoning atmosphere.

Although she is steeped in the traditions of classic French cuisine and imbued with a great respect for and understanding of seventeeth-century gastronomy, Miss Toklas represents an extraordinary innovation—that is typically twentieth century. At the same time an intellectual, an epicure and a practical cook, she can cook at the same high level of perfection as she talks and writes about food.

This is a new development in the gastronomic world. Always before in the history of epicureanism, the performer and the critic or appreciator of the art have been different people. It is quite possible that neither Lucullus nor Madame Pompadour could boil an egg. This inability did not detract, of course, from their sensitive virtuosity.

It remained for America, however, to combine performance

with appreciation. It remained for an American to become a kind of symbol of this new combination of epicure and cook.

Despite her long residence in Paris, Alice Toklas remains essentially an American. Without chauvinism, she is inclined to agree with Gertrude Stein that "The United States is the oldest country in the world because it was the first to enter the 20th century."

What began in the United States is spreading now to other countries. Through a curious juxtaposition of influences—through wars, social upheavals, the disappearance of servants—the twentieth century has produced an epicure who is creator as well as critic. It has also produced a yearning and a need for a more intellectual approach to cooking.

Cooking with the Mind

There is a possibility that Gertrude Stein might not have approved our new combination of artist and critic. For on the subject of drawing she once wrote, "It is a good thing to have no sense of how it is done in the things that amuse you. You should have one absorbing occupation, and as for other things in life for full enjoyment you should only contemplate results. In this way you are bound to feel more about it than those who know a little of how it is done."

Unfortunately or perhaps fortunately not many women in the modern world are permitted the luxury of merely contemplating or enjoying good food without knowledge of how it is done. Perhaps Gertrude Stein's observation was not intended to apply to matters gastronomical. I have heard Alice Toklas remark that it adds much delight to a dish to know the recipe or at least to know the technique of it and to be able to guess or try to guess what the special flavorings may be and what particular quirks of technique give its individual quality.

Not only in eating but also in cooking the mind plays an important role. Perhaps it is the greatest contribution of Alice Toklas that she brings good thinking and a well-stocked memory to the cook stove. In history there have been many scholarly epicures and many epicurean scholars. Rarely have the two been combined as she has combined them.

Alice Toklas is the exponent and the prototype of the intellectual cook. At this moment of history this is a matter of considerable significance, since millions of well-educated persons, men and women, are faced especially in the United States with the need to do chores that could be dull and depressing or tremendously stimulating—depending upon the point of view.

Perhaps the way of Alice B. Toklas is the way out—the liberation—for these women in America who are being forced willy-nilly into what might be the arid isolation of housework and child-raising. This desert often extends through a number of years while children are young. For it is not true that our modern mechanical appliances free women from domestic responsibilities. They help to make her more efficient but at the same time they load upon her more responsibilities, rather than fewer. They make it possible for her to do more and more. But more and more is being required of her.

A lively-minded young woman of the upper middle classes would, in her grandmother's or even her mother's day, have had a servant or possibly two. She would have been helped with the cooking, nursing the children and cleaning the house. There were the friendly grocer, the helpful butcher to guide and reassure her. Knowledgeable relatives and older neighbors gave her the benefit of their experience. But now there is little help other than what is mechanical and packaged. The harried wife of a well-paid executive said wistfully the other day, "I'd give up all my mechanical servants—all of them happily for one good old-fashioned maid-of-all-work. Like the one we had when I was a child!"

Helping hands are not, by any means, our only lack. What we need even more is personalized advice. We have newspapers, magazines, radio, television, package directions, plenty of advice of one kind, but all of it is geared for everyone. None of it is personal. The impersonal supermarket can give no thought to an individual dilemma. Houses are too small for relatives, and building developments are more and more likely to include only one age group.

There is only one sure way to cope with this problem. It is the way that humanity has coped most successfully throughout history. By using our heads! Through the exercise of intellect—by paying more rather than less attention to domesticity we can make it more interesting and rewarding. The one facet of everyday living that responds most abundantly to this approach is cooking. Exquisite and thoughtful cooking in the Alice B. Toklas tradition will not only exercise but also appeal to the mind. What is more, it lifts the heart and stimulates the spirit.

A Life-Taught Cook

Like so many others in America, Alice B. Toklas is a self-taught, life-taught cook. It is recorded in the *Autobiography* that she was born in San Francisco. Her mother's father was a pioneer who arrived in California during the gold rush of '49. Her father came of Polish patriotic stock and her main interests, to quote again, have always been needlework, gardening, pictures, of course, furniture, tapestry, houses, flowers. Much as she has loved flowers, she appreciates even more vegetables, fruit trees and all sorts of things that are in any way connected with cooking. Coming as she did from a well-to-do household, properly staffed even for elaborate entertainment, she learned early to be an epicure. But not until many years later, after she had come to live in Paris with Gertrude Stein, did she begin to take real notice and to cook, herself.

Already she had a collection of recipes. With her the recipes came before the actual practice of cooking. Several times during her mother's absences, she had in her girlhood taken over the running of the household and the ordering of the meals. She began to note the recipes of some of her favorite dishes. Some were recipes of friends; many came from cooks. In France she kept the recipes she gathered in a cardboard box and later added those from England, Italy and Spain. The box endured and out-lasted the German occupation.

Generally she remembers all about each recipe, where she first tasted it, who wrote it for her. But sometimes the background has slipped away out of memory and she will say of a certain dish only that "it comes from the box."

Whatever the origin of her recipes, Alice Toklas brings to them something valuable in the way of understanding, appreciation and interpretation. Her intellectual and philosophical attitude toward cooking is expressed in the *Autobiography*. For instance, she speaks of Matisse, "who frequently used his distorted drawing as a dissonance is used in music or as vinegar or lemons are used in cooking or egg shells in coffee to clarify. . . ."

She goes on to say, "I do inevitably take my comparisons from the kitchen because I like food and cooking and know something about it."

The Legend and the Lady

It was in April of 1953 that Elizabeth Gordon, editor of *House Beautiful*, invited Alice Toklas to come from Paris to Venice to join us for at least a part of a gastronomical reporting trip through northern Italy. She had given a glowingly savory account of miraculous luncheons that Miss Toklas had cooked for her in the apartment on the Left Bank, but, as I remember, she had not described the person. The only pictures in my mind were those I had gleaned from reading and from conversation with some friends who had met her. She was someone who cared about extraordinary hats. A big black hat with a lovely yellow feather trimming was described in the *Autobiography*. And I also remember that someone had seen her wearing a black waistcoat at the Opéra.

At any rate, I was completely unprepared for the person we found waiting for us at the Royal Danieli in Venice. With her usual courtly punctuality, Alice Toklas had arrived at exactly the hour agreed upon. We were a little late. So she was waiting.

A small, regal figure scarcely five feet tall, in a gray suit tailored but not too strictly tailored (as I know now by their protégé Pierre Balmain). The suit had a long jacket most appropriate for the Edwardian lady that she is. The buttons were eighteenth-century cut steel.

All these details came much later. The first feeling was about her eyes. It is not only that they are large but that they are so bright, giving out sparks. When she is about to say something especially wise or critical or amusing, she telegraphs it first with her eyes. Although when I met her she was already close to eighty, her hair was still not too gray but gave an impression of darkness. It was cut short, almost but not quite cropped—in a manner that would become widely fashionable within a year or two.

Over her forehead there were bangs faintly echoed by a dark down over her lip which, as one of her friends has put it, makes other faces seem nude by comparison.

Her blouse was of a heavy white silk, tailored, impeccable and beautifully sewn. There was, as there is generally, a brooch at her throat, rather large and curiously wrought. All her brooches have their own story. Her gloves were Paris perfection but her small feet were unexpected—in flat leather sandals like those Isadora Duncan used to wear.

She had in her hand a slender, tightly rolled and jacketed umbrella. Usually she has it with her but leans on it only occasionally and lightly. That day I noticed especially the scent she wore. It was light, elegant, unfamiliar—so fashionably new that it had not yet come to the United States. A highly suitable scent, Jolie Madame, also from Balmain.

What was most extraordinary was and is the way that despite her tiny figure she can dominate a room, a group, a conversation. In the most fashionable places, like Maxim's or Le Moutière at Saint Germain or at dinner parties among the greats of the Cognac or the Champagne country where we have been together, all heads turn toward her. No matter how softly or how slowly she speaks, everyone listens. A whole party knots around her.

Nothing escapes her analytical attention—nothing about the relationships of people. Never a single nuance is disregarded concerning the food and the wine. Her memory of fragrance and taste is so well developed that years afterward she can recall and often re-create a dish that she has tasted only once.

A Continuing Colloquy

Almost immediately, within an hour or two, after our first meeting in Venice there began between Alice Toklas and me a conversation about food and cooking that has continued by word and letter for years. She began it by telling me that while she enjoyed reading my articles in *House Beautiful* on the subject of the modern epicure she disagreed with me about almost everything and particularly with my basic belief that it is possible to be an epicure, even an epicure-cook, in a hurry.

Between speed and ease and excellence there could be, she felt, no possible connection. All processed or prepared foods, canned, packaged or (horror of horrors!) frozen, were to be regarded not only with suspicion but disdain. In gondolas and galleries, in churches, in palaces, in markets, antique shops, cafés and automobiles, our colloquy continued.

One of the subjects to which we returned over and over again in talk and later in letters was the American mix and particularly the cake mix. At first she scathed them all. There was a cheap and easy vulgarity about them. Lean yet curiously fatted, with some peculiar substances certainly not butter. The flavorings were too much and synthetic. There was too much salt.

She admitted that she had tried or tasted only a few of them and those not for a long time.

I agreed that there had been and still were many poor ones and that even among the best there were imperfections.

"If I bring them to you, will you try and see for yourself?"

She agreed that this was only fair.

So the day before I flew to France I gathered together a dozen mixes—two of each, a whole suitcase full. I was packing them when the Ralph Bunches came to say good-by and to give me a little wedding gift to carry along for Gunnar Myrdal's daughter.

"What are those?" they asked.

"They're cake mixes," I said.

"And you're taking them to Paris?"

"They're for Alice Toklas. She's a very great cook," I said, "and she hates mixes, so I'm taking them to her."

No one could blame Dr. Bunche for looking dazed. "I'm sure that makes a lot of sense," he said, "but I don't quite understand it."

It would have been lengthy and a little difficult to explain. The kindly officials of Air France who met me at Orly Airport were even more puzzled. The Customs man peered at the packages with unbelieving eyes. "Is madame afraid perhaps that she will starve in Paris?"

Nevertheless it was a worth-while experiment. A month or so after my return to the States came her letter, written in the fine precise handwriting which looks for all the world like the most delicate lace.

"About the mixes, I've had huge success with the yellow cake. It is perfect. I've made two half packages and one big one. My oven doesn't hold two layer tins. They were all baked in square tins, cut in half when cold and filled with butter cream, one curaçao-flavored and the icing flavored with Drambuie. One was filled and iced with rum-flavored cream. One had in the center a layer of finely chopped crystallized apricots, pineapples, plums and oranges all covered with kirsch-flavored cream and kirsch in the frosting. The devil's food cake was equally successful. The first time filled with fluffy chocolate icing and covered with it. Excellent but difficult to serve—not suitable for tea. So since then I've made them as little cakes, filled them with mocha cream in the center. The icing was chocolate and another time praline cream and praline icing. Delicious!

"There's no way to express my conversion to these two mixes. The ginger bread too."

A popover mix to which I am passionately devoted fared less well. I have always contended that a special type of flour used in the mix practically guarantees success even under the most trying circumstances.

But Alice wrote, "There's little time saving with the popover mix and I am a successful popover-maker."

The angel-cake mix and the biscuit mix frightened her. "Next week," she said, "I am going to take my courage and go to the angel cake." It was startling to hear from her, a long time afterward, that she who could achieve some of the most elaborate and painstaking dishes in all the world had never had the fortitude to attempt an angel cake. As far as I know she never did, not even with the mix. Perhaps it was a relic from the childhood days in San Francisco when only the most competent and the most experienced would assay it.

Although she remains staunchly American in spite of fifty years in France, you have the feeling sometimes that she has forgotten some of our more colloquial eating habits. The hot baking-powder-biscuit mix did not intrigue her. She referred to it in her letter as the "yeast" biscuits and said, "They can't save more than ten minutes, is that worth while?"

Probably it would be if you hanker for them often. Ten minutes and ten minutes and ten minutes. They do mount up. Still, it is a good question to ask or to have someone ask for you. And this is one of the great contributions of an Alice Toklas that she asks so many and so many right questions.

She Bows to the Blender

If Miss Toklas' conversion to mixes was limited and with reservations, her first swift and real enthusiasm was reserved for the electric blender. Until the blender came into her life she had not been willing to use any of the modern short cuts—either products or appliances—because she felt they subtracted from perfection. But after she had used it for a few weeks she wrote an article which she called "A Blessed Blender in the Home":

"Do the good friends who sent me the electric blender possibly realize to what an extent it has revolutionized my daily life and liberated me from the struggle of finding time to do what must be done and give me the compensating hours to do what I want to do . . . ? For them the blender is a reality; for me it is a miracle. Now that it has been my most precious possession for several months, it has taught me two important things, that it is possible to prepare with it most of the great French dishes in no more time than it does the simplest of food without it and that it permits me to cook, to serve and to be free to remain at table with one's guests."

She goes on to exclaim that "tomato juice after one or two minutes in the blender comes from a celestial sphere. It is marvelous as a sauce to spoon over young spring lettuces."

Actually such tomato juice, or, more accurately, finely puréed tomato, is not at all the same as the beverage we know. It is thick, foamy, rose-pink rather than red. Just as she suggests it is better suited for spooning than for sipping.

Out of her epicurean imagination came a blender-inspired fruit dessert, "a single fruit or combination of peaches and strawberries in equal parts or pears or raspberries, preferably unsweetened, a tablespoon of kirsch or any liqueur of your choice may be added." She suggests serving it with whipped cream. For me it needs no topping.

With the blender Alice Toklas makes quenelles, those delicate poached morsels of fish chopped incredibly fine when raw. These are acknowledged to be one of France's greatest dishes. Also she makes the sauce royale to go along with it. (See pages 29 and 30.)

She evolves a salmon soufflé and a perfect shrimp sauce. Leg of mutton Sultana (page 52), an extraordinary crab bisque, stuffed breast of veal and stuffed duck. Her blended meat loaf, which is more of a pâté than the usual meat loaf, is exceedingly fine and smooth in texture.

From currant or raspberry jelly, cream cheese and egg whites comes a delectable version of slip-and-go-easy (page 128).

Blissfully Breaking Rules

Before the blender was dispatched to Paris there were several long conversations and some letters that went along with the regulation recipe book to acquaint Miss Toklas with the rules for its use. She was exhorted not to use the blender to whip cream or submit egg whites to its fast-whirling action. The cream would curdle, the egg whites would "cook." Blandly she ignored the rulings and sent me a recipe for a chocolate mousse as luscious as the one they serve at Gaffner's, which means that it is just about as luxurious as any in the whole, wide world. As you can see on page 122, the egg whites and the cream go blithely into the blender. I was sure that she had made a mistake. I tried the recipe in the approved manner, and then I tried it her way. I shall never forget my husband's comment: "Hers tastes real, exactly as I remember it from Paris. My dear, I am sorry to say yours is a puffy home-economics version."

Since that time, bans upon the blender have been lifted. In our laboratories and test kitchens we have discovered that there are ways and times when many more things are possible than were dreamed of in our previous strait-laced philosophy. But Alice Toklas learned these things within a few hours and in the most inconvenient kitchen extant!

Creative (?) Cooking

But if Miss Toklas has been even in some measure converted to mixes and blenders, there has been conversion on the other side too. The question of "creative cooking," for instance! For me it has always been the highest accolade to achieve imaginative originality. I shall not forget her snort of scorn when I used the phrase "creative cooking"! Her voice and her eyebrows rose, questioning "What would that be?" And I was forced to admit that the inventions and improvisations of many untutored cooks could be abominable. I who wanted to do everything a new way began to catch at least a glimmering of the classical French attitude.

Little by little I began to understand that there can be value in giving fine performance of another's composition . . . that an exquisite interpretation can be in its own way just as creative, just as imaginative as an invention. I began to comprehend a little the French resentment against change without reason. It began to dawn upon me that certain dishes, like sonnets or odes, cannot be brought into being without obeisance to classic rules and restrictions.

Alice Toklas, of course, does not represent the extreme authoritarian point of view. She says of the French, "They like to say that their food stems from culture and that it has developed over the centuries. . . . Foreigners living in France respect and appreciate this point of view, but deplore their too strict observance of a tradition which will not admit of the slightest deviation in a seasoning or the suppression of a single ingredient." She does deplore that a dish as simple as a potato salad must always be served surrounded by chicory and that to serve it with any other green is inconceivable. But on the other hand she admits that such strict conservative attitudes over the years have resulted in the evolution of a number of essential principles that have made the renown of the French cuisine.

The French concern for tradition and seasonability can also result in some quite distressing monotony. I do remember that from Alice Toklas, too, there was a small murmur of disapproval when in the strawberry season we were hospitably proffered by our hosts and hostesses strawberries—beautiful, luscious, fragrant, but strawberries, strawberries—twelve times in six consecutive days.

Another time at luncheon Elizabeth Gordon and I were exulting, a little chauvinistically perhaps, about the riches of the American larder. "With our traditions and in our menus we can now *cream* the world for our tables. We can have a Russian soup, a Chinese vegetable with our American steak and follow it with a French dessert."

"How incongruous!" Alice Toklas said softly.

We were, it is true, somewhat dashed. We still believe that, as citizens of the world, we have a right to make such juxtapositions. But now we realize that artfulness is required to make a merger of widely divergent elements. We know, too, that there is another point of view.

We understand why some French visitors say of our food that it is "too highly seasoned" . . . "too imaginative" . . . "too mixed up" . . . "One menu is a potpourri from a dozen countries" . . . "Exotic and yet at the same time somehow savorless" . . . "Everything tastes as if it had been washed in ice water". . . .

Certainly there are some unusual ingredients in Alice Toklas' cooking. Perhaps the most talk-provoking recipe of the decade was the marijuana fudge which appeared in the English but not the American edition of *The Alice B. Toklas Cook Book* in a chapter among the recipes of her friends. But the essential characteristic of her cooking is far from esoteric. If it can be put into a phrase, it is a meticulous regard for detail and nuance.

At the luncheons that she cooked for us in Paris (we came at twelve-thirty—we stayed till five) there was nothing strange. First sherry in the salon and a tray of crisp small crackers spread moments before with a cognac-scented pâté of chicken livers. For an entrée, asparagus with buttered crumbs. Nothing at all peculiar about them except that these were the wild stalks no thicker than darning thread. To get them had meant a trip at dawn to a market stall in Les Halles. Or another time, to introduce the meal, nothing but scrambled eggs, one might say. But hers was a recipe she had from Picabia; the eggs are mated with almost equal parts of butter and softly seethed for almost an hour till they set into a golden cream. And afterward, perhaps a leg of lamb so infant that the whole gigot is not much longer than your hand.

Each morsel must, in the Toklas tradition, be perfect of its kind, chosen and prepared with love, understanding and erudition.

About This Book

In the attitudes of both of us there had been many changes between the spring of 1953, when we first met in Venice, and the autumn of 1957, when it was decided that I should help with the editing of Alice Toklas' second cook book. Almost unconsciously I had adopted many of her ideas. And she, instead of disagreeing as she had before, had decided that what I wrote was "not only interesting but woman-of-the-worldly."

My first awe of her remained but in addition I had a great admiring affection for her. The hours we spent together over the manuscript were for me, at least, an unalloyed delight as well as an introduction to gastronomic wisdom of the highest order.

On several occasions we worked in my rooms at the Plaza-Athénée in what we called the Boat Suite, which is really a series of tiny maids' rooms that have been remodeled to look like quarters on a yacht—a yacht moored among the rooftops of Paris with a breath-taking view of constantly changing clouds around the Eiffel Tower! Basil, the courtly Russian floor waiter, brought our lunches. On the day we finished we celebrated with lobster soufflé. And a Corton Charlemagne 1952! At least twice we worked ten hours at a stretch. I was the one who suggested stopping. Miss Toklas showed no signs of weariness. In all things she is so disciplined.

Mostly we worked at her apartment on the Left Bank, close to the Odéon. It is not the apartment of the Rue de Fleurus that was described in the *Autobiography* but it could well be. There is the same Italian Renaissance furniture. The same high ceilings, the walls covered in the same way from floor to frieze with unframed paintings by Picasso, Juan Gris, Francis Rose, Matisse. They are in the halls, in the dining room and the salon. Here and there, however, nowadays there are vacant, pale, bare squares and rectangles that mark the places where a loan has already been delivered to some institution or museum. Ultimately they will all go.

This was a romantic if not too comfortable setting for work on a cook book. The gaze of Picasso's harlequins was upon us—priceless examples of his rose and blue periods. We talked about the proper way to stew apples and how stewed apples are different from compote while our eyes rested upon the green apple that Picasso had painted for Gertrude Stein.

It was cold and gray in Paris in November. We sat beside a seventeenth-century mantel of polished white marble. But the fireplace has been boarded up for a hundred years. The house is much too old, the chimneys much too crumbly to permit a fire. Heat comes stingily from a kerosene-burning stove shaped like an old-fashioned wash boiler. It gives out headachy fumes. Nevertheless it is a lovely room full of treasures and remembering.

We spread our notes and papers over the sofa upholstered in horsehair, the natural color of a shining bay mare, and on the two small slipper chairs which Gertrude Stein embroidered in petit-point over designs drawn by one of their more frequent dinner guests—one Pablo Picasso.

No Lavender or Old Lace

Nothing in their apartment has changed since Gertrude Stein died in 1946. The past is immanent there—indwelling, inherent. But it would be a great mistake to assume any sentimentality in the atmosphere or the attitudes of Alice B. Toklas. The sweetness-and-light school of thought and expression are completely alien. She bristles, sparkles, crackles, lashes out—especially when the subject is food and the object of her ire is the penciled editorial corrections, suggestions and questions in the margin of her manuscript.

"How many does this recipe serve?"

"How should I know how many it serves? It depends—on their appetites—what else they have for dinner—whether they like it or not."

In some cases we compromised by giving the quantities that

might be expected to be produced when the recipe was finished. How many cupfuls and what amounts would make a respectable portion?

"Such questions," she burst out. "Typically home economics . . ." Her exasperation flared. "They are so finicky," she said, "but not thorough. There's a difference."

In many of her recipes, especially for cakes, you will see that she says "stir." Almost always the editor had changed "stir" to "beat" but Miss Toklas said, "Change it right back. It is not the same thing. Stirring is a round-and-round motion, beating is up, down and around. Experience has shown that the end result, the taste and the texture, are quite different. The physicists could probably tell us why."

Over and over again there appeared in the margin the notation "Salt ? ? ?" Miss Toklas had not forgotten the salt. The omission, when it occurs, is deliberate. Salt does not appear automatically in all European recipes. She is distressed to find that in America the pinch of salt has become routine even in desserts. "Sometimes you need it, sometimes you don't. It is a matter to be considered and thought about."

She told me a story about herself as a little girl and how she placed her finger tip in the salt dish and put it to her lips. "Salt has a lovely taste. I thought so then, I still think so—a lovely individual taste of its own that should be appreciated, not become merely a matter of course. We Americans kill the taste of salt by using too much."

Another question often in the margin: "How do you serve this? With rice?"

"Have we gone mad about rice back home?" she wanted to know. She sees no reason why an entrée should be served *with* or *on* anything. "You mustn't be afraid to serve things alone on their own. . . . But of course there is bread on the table."

On the subject of economy Miss Toklas shows a dual personality. She shares the French sense of thrift, wasting nothing, saving the bones, using the shells of shrimp and the scrapings under the shells of lobsters to enrich her bisques and sauces. As is the custom in that country of little refrigeration and still practically no quick freezing, she markets frugally in small quantities. But her use of ingredients is lavish. About wines, she says: "The better the wine the better the dish. There are no exceptions. Whenever I say sherry, I mean dry sherry. Even in desserts I use a fine dry pale fino sherry or an Amontillado, and if it is needed perhaps a little more sugar. I never expect the sherry to supply the sweetness."

The Mood and the Method

The recipes in this book have not been changed, edited or adapted in any way. They appear just as Miss Toklas wrote them. But there are, set apart in different type, a few addenda that will, I hope, make them easier to understand and to use in the United States. With each recipe there is a listing of the principal ingredients that you will need. When products are not easy to find in the United States, substitutions have been suggested. And there are a few thoughts on ways in which these dishes can be used to enhance the meals of Now and Here.

In this book you will find the flavors and aromas of past and present, the moods and the methods of yesterday and today serenely merged into Exquisite Cooking.

Very few people are indifferent to either the aroma or flavor of garlic. One is affected favorably or unfavorably. It may have been the odor of garlic with which Henry James was greeted when he went to call upon George Eliot for the first time and which he later described as the right odor in the wrong place.

Though I had not tasted garlic as a young girl when I read this, it had the alluring mysterious quality of the unknown for some years after. Then I was asked to a lunch party at a schoolmate's. Upon my return my mother asked me if I had enjoyed myself. Inexpressibly, I breathed. For lunch there was steak smothered in garlic. It was to be a long time before I was to know such rapture and surprise again. For garlic was not admitted in my mother's kitchen, nor did she consider my enjoyment of the strong flavor of salmon, sweetbreads, Brussel sprouts, all cheeses, caviar, the onion family including garlic, and wine, natural or commendable in her young daughter. But these are all as enjoyable to me today as they were then.

The more pronounced the odor and the taste, the less necessity is there to add any other to them—a single herb perhaps to accentuate their flavor. The present overindulgence in herbs stems from the meat restriction during the war years when they suggested more meat than we had. And now they are used indiscreetly, indiscriminately, and the result is a sad mésalliance and disturbed memory.

One longs to return to a few simple herbs with an unjaded palate. The French use with discretion a mild mixture which they call Four Spices, composed of pepper, ginger, cloves and nutmeg, and which varies in its proportions. In any case, spices should be bought in small quantities, for they don't retain their flavor even when well cooked.

Since these are recipes that I recommend it is perhaps pardonable to commence with a word of explanation, if not of caution.

First, quality. Use only the best the market offers. If the budget is restricted, restrict the menu to what the budget affords. Cook with the very best butter, draw on your best wines to flavor a common piece of meat or of fish. This will exalt your effort, stimulate, intensify, indeed magnify the flavor. Your appreciation and appetite will increase. You will add to the pleasure of your guests.

And secondly. Consider the menus carefully, that there is a harmony and a suitable progression, as you do for the arrangement of a bouquet or of the planting of a bed of flowers. In the menu there should be a climax and a culmination. Come to it gently. One will suffice.

White Soup of Artichokes

A package of frozen artichoke hearts and a can of Swanson's chicken broth make an admirable version of this soup. If you use a blender you needn't bother about sieving or straining.

YOU WILL NEED:
>Artichokes
>Chicken bouillon
>Thin cream

Cut 1 pound artichokes into small pieces and boil with 1½ cups chicken bouillon in covered saucepan for ½ hour. Strain through fine sieve. Return to heat and add 2 cups thin cream. Do not boil but serve hot.

Cold Pink Consommé

This is one recipe where you can't use the blender. You need a fine sieve to remove the seeds and skin.

YOU WILL NEED:
>Tomatoes
>Chicken bouillon
>Heavy cream

For 4 persons simmer 4 ripe tomatoes in 6 cups good chicken bouillon over low flame for ½ hour. Strain through hair sieve and add 4 tablespoons heavy cream.

Russian Soup

This recipe makes 6 servings.

YOU WILL NEED: *Bouillon*
    Flour   *Salt*
    Eggs   *Pepper*

For 4 persons stir 1 cup flour with the yolks of 2 eggs and 1 whole egg until perfectly smooth. Add ½ cup bouillon, ½ teaspoon salt and ¼ teaspoon pepper. Drop by teaspoonfuls into 5 cups boiling bouillon and cook for 12 minutes over medium heat. Serve very hot.

Soup à la Cardinale

This is an extraordinary—extraordinarily good, novel, nourishing and sustaining—soup, bursting, in case you care, with all manner of high-type proteins and vitamins. If you like, instead of chopping the liver you may cut it into cubes and put it into the blender along with a scant cup of beef bouillon. Makes 6 hearty servings.

YOU WILL NEED:
    Calf's liver   *Parsley*
    Butter   *Cinnamon*
    Bread   *Nutmeg*
    Parmesan cheese   *Salt*
    Beef bouillon   *Powdered hazel nuts*

Sauté ½ pound calf's liver in 2 tablespoons butter. Chop fine. Toast 4 slices of bread, place in soup tureen, sprinkle with ¾ cup grated Parmesan cheese and the chopped liver. Heat 5 cups good beef bouillon, add ½ tablespoon parsley, a pinch of cinnamon, a pinch of nutmeg, 1 teaspoon salt and 2 tablespoons powdered hazel nuts. Bring to a boil and pour into soup tureen.

Mulligatawny Soup

YOU WILL NEED:

Chicken	Mushrooms
Veal or chicken bouillon	Mace
Carrots	Cardamom
Onions	Cinnamon stick
Cloves	Butter
Leek	Cornstarch
Celery	Curry
	Heavy cream

This is a meal in itself to be served with an excellent Madeira or dry sherry.

Put in the soup pot a large fine chicken cut in joints as for a fricassee. Over a high flame pour 4 cups veal or chicken bouillon over the chicken. Skim carefully, lower heat and skim until no more scum forms. Then add 2 sliced carrots, 1 onion stuck with 2 cloves, 1 sliced leek, the outside pieces and leaves of a celery, 5 or 6 sliced mushrooms, 2 blades of mace, 1 tablespoon crushed cardamom seeds and 1-inch stick of cinnamon. Cover and simmer for 2 hours.

In the meantime prepare this velouté. Cook 1 chopped onion in 2 tablespoons butter over very low flame. When it is cooked remove from flame. Slowly dilute 1 tablespoon cornstarch with 1½ cups of the bouillon from the chicken, add 1 teaspoon good curry. Simmer for 10 minutes. Then strain the soup and add the diluted cornstarch. Add ¾ cup heavy cream. When the chicken is arch-tender place the pieces in the tureen, cover with the thickened bouillon and serve.

Soup au Pistou

YOU WILL NEED:

String beans	Leek
Green peas	Carrot

White cabbage	Bouquet including fresh or
Potatoes	powdered basil
Tomato	Elbow macaroni
Salt	Garlic
Cayenne	Parmesan cheese

This is one of the Provençal recipes that came from Genoa to Nice when Savoy belonged to Italy, now nearly a hundred years ago. It is nourishing, satisfying and quickly prepared.

For 4 persons cook 1 cup string beans cut in 1-inch lengths, 1 cup green peas, 1 leek, 1 carrot, ½ white cabbage, 2 sliced potatoes and 1 skinned tomato in 2 quarts water with 1½ teaspoon salt, a pinch of cayenne, and a bouquet including fresh basil, or 1 teaspoon powdered basil. Boil covered for 20 minutes. Then add ¾ cup elbow macaroni. Lower heat to prevent macaroni from attaching to bottom of pan. Cook for 12 minutes, then add 3 cloves of crushed garlic. Pour into tureen with ½ cup grated Parmesan cheese. Serve with additional grated Parmesan cheese in a bowl.

This is one of the glories of the Provençal cuisine. They say it can only be cooked in summer when fresh basil and string beans are in season, but now that the winter has come I have found that tinned beans and powdered basil make highly satisfactory substitutes.

Bourride, or Fish Soup

YOU WILL NEED:	Tomato
Eel	Green pepper
Red mullet	Bay leaf
Whiting	Fennel
Turbot	Thyme
Olive oil	Clove
Onions	Orange peel
Shallots	Salt
Garlic	Soft-shell crabs

Saffron   Parsley
Cayenne   Parmesan cheese
French bread   Rouille sauce

This too is a Provençal soup.

For 4 persons take 4 pounds of fish: eel, red mullet, whiting and turbot, if possible. Clean the fish; remove fins but leave the heads; slice. Place 3 tablespoons olive oil in large saucepan with 3 large sliced onions, 2 shallots, 3 cloves garlic, 1 sliced tomato, 1 sliced green pepper, 1 bay leaf, 2 slices fennel and 1 twig of thyme. When these are hot add ½ cup olive oil, 1 clove, ¼ orange peel, 1 tablespoon salt and 8 cups hot water, the sliced fish and 4 soft-shell crabs. Cover and boil for 15 minutes. Remove fish and crabs and keep hot. Add a good pinch of saffron and a small pinch of cayenne. Place slices of French bread about ½ inch thick in deep dish. Place fish upon them, pour boiling, strained fish bouillon upon them. Sprinkle with 1 tablespoon chopped parsley. Serve with grated Parmesan cheese and a rouille sauce (see page 101).

Crab Bisque

YOU WILL NEED: Butter
    Crab   Sugar
    Carrots   Chicken bouillon
    Onion   Dry white wine
    Celery   Cognac
    Sea salt   Lean ham
    Peppercorns   Boiled rice
    Bay leaf   Heavy cream
    Thyme   Croutons

Clean the crab thoroughly by brushing with a stiff brush and rinsing frequently in running water. Be certain that all dirt and sand are removed. Prepare a court bouillon with 3 sliced carrots, 1 sliced onion, ½ head celery, ½ teaspoon sea salt, 5 whole peppercorns, 1 bay leaf and a twig of thyme. Place these in an enameled pot over medium heat with 2 tablespoons butter, a pinch of sugar, and once again a bay leaf and a twig of thyme. Stir with a wooden spoon until this turns golden brown, then add 1 cup chicken bouillon, 1 cup dry white wine, 1 liqueur glass of cognac, ½ pound lean ham cut in small pieces and enough water to cover the crab—about 4 cups for a medium-size crab. When this boils put the crab in the pot, cover and boil for 20 minutes. Remove from pot and drain. Strain the court bouillon. Put the vegetables and ham aside, crack the crab and remove all the meat from the body and the claws. Put the crab meat and the ham and vegetables in the blender along with the strained bouillon and 2 cups boiled rice. Blend first at low speed, then at high speed until smooth and very fine. Then place in a saucepan and add 1 cup heavy cream. Put over medium heat and when about to boil add 2 tablespoons butter cut in small pieces. Do not allow to boil and do not stir, but tip in all directions. Serve with small unbuttered croutons.

BISCUITS AND DUMPLINGS

Savory Biscuits

These cheese biscuits flavored with curry, dry mustard and a touch of cayenne would be an interesting bouchée to serve with cocktails, soup or salad. In America we would probably prefer them piping hot though Miss Toklas suggests that they should be tepid or cold.

Her recipe does not call for baking powder but if you like a fluffier texture you may use 2 teaspoons of the cream-of-tartar type or 1 teaspoon of double-acting baking powder.

Makes about 18 small biscuits.

YOU WILL NEED:
- Butter
- Flour
- Grated cheese
- Egg
- Milk
- Curry powder
- Dry mustard
- Salt
- Cayenne pepper

Rub ¼ cup butter into ¾ cup sifted flour. Add ½ cup grated cheese, 1 beaten egg mixed with 1 tablespoon milk, ½ teaspoon curry powder, ¼ teaspoon dry mustard, ¼ teaspoon salt and a pinch of cayenne. Roll this on lightly floured board. Cut with cookie cutter and place on lightly buttered cookie sheet. Bake until pale gold in 400° oven. Serve tepid or cold.

Miss Lindley's Cream Muffins

(KINDNESS OF MR. EUGENE WALTER)

Here again you will find no baking powder, only cream, eggs and flour, and note that the eggs are stirred, not beaten. Half fill buttered muffin tins or patty pans. Makes about 20 muffins.

7

YOU WILL NEED:
    Cream   Flour
    Eggs   Butter
Mix 1 cup cream with the stirred yolks of 2 eggs. Add 1 cup sifted flour. Beat until perfectly smooth. Then gently fold in the beaten whites of 2 eggs. Bake in well-buttered patty pans for 12 minutes in 425° oven.

Out of this world!

Shortcake Biscuits

(KINDNESS OF MR. EUGENE WALTER)

Imagine a shortcake made with these biscuits and covered with tiny wild strawberries or raspberries, so fresh from the garden that they still carry the original aroma of roses!

In Paris they would serve crème fraîche, which despite the name is not fresh at all but pale yellow gold with a lift of sour. Our snowy-white, commercially soured cream makes an admirable adjunct to a shortcake. If you want the cream to have the look of Paris you can stir in an egg yolk.

The recipe makes about 20 small shortcakes.

YOU WILL NEED: Sugar
    Flour   Salt
    Baking powder   Butter
Sift 1½ cups flour. Sift again with 2½ teaspoons baking powder, 2 tablespoons sugar and a pinch of salt. Cut in ¼ cup butter until there are no lumps larger than a small green pea. Add ⅓ to ½ cup ice water, just enough to roll. Roll on lightly floured board to ½-inch thickness. Cut with small cookie cutter and place on lightly buttered baking sheet. Paint them with melted butter and bake in 450° oven for 10 minutes.

Mimi Cake

A surprising recipe, perhaps; no baking powder, no eggs, just flour, cream and a touch of salt, like a bannock or corn pone . . . to serve hot, tepid or cold, not with dessert but with cheese, soup or salad.

YOU WILL NEED:
> *Flour*
> *Heavy cream*
> *Salt*

This is called cake but they are distinctly biscuits.

Mix 1 cup sifted flour with 1 cup heavy cream and a pinch of salt until the dough is perfectly smooth. Roll out and place on a square shallow cake tin. Bake in a 250° oven until pale gold. Remove from pan and cut in squares.

Corn-Flour Cake

This is a kind of corn pone or refined johnnycake. In the old days in our South it would have held the imprint of the fingers that flattened it. The corn flour to which Miss Toklas refers we would call corn meal. White or yellow corn meal may be used—preferably stone ground. The flavor is more delicate.

YOU WILL NEED:
> *Corn flour or finely ground white corn meal*
> *White flour*
> *Sugar*
> *Butter*

Thoroughly mix ½ cup sifted corn flour with ¾ cup sifted white flour and 1 cup sugar. Add 1 cup melted butter and mix until perfectly even. Flatten into a square or oblong cake pan and bake in a 325° oven until a pale golden color. Remove from tin, cut into squares and serve hot, tepid or cold.

Polish Dumplings

When the dough is cut in 2-inch squares, this recipe makes about 3 dozen dumplings.

YOU WILL NEED: Butter
    Flour   *Sour cream*
    Eggs   *Cottage cheese*

Work 2 cups sifted flour into the slightly beaten yolks of 3 eggs. Add just enough water to make a stiff dough that does not stick to either your hands or the pastry board. The dough must be satin smooth. Chill for 20 minutes. Roll very, very thin. Cut with a cookie cutter or with a knife into squares. Have a large saucepan of boiling water. Drop the squares into it. They will rise as soon as they are done. Remove with a perforated spoon. Rinse in cold water. Drain thoroughly. Brown in very hot butter in skillet on both sides. When golden brown remove from skillet and sprinkle over them ½ cup heavy sour cream and ½ cup crumbled cottage cheese. Serve very hot.

Eggs à l'Hypocras

At first glance this recipe may seem surprising—eggs with wine, vinegar and spices. But the taste is not too different from the pickled eggs which many Americans have savored all their lives as a great picnic treat. An interesting first course for a summer dinner or entrée for lunch or supper.

YOU WILL NEED:
Eggs
Batter for frying
Vin rosé
White wine vinegar
Honey
Cloves
Stick cinnamon
Salt
Cayenne
Cognac
Clarified butter

In 1656 Hypocras recommended eggs cooked in this manner as health-giving.

Hard-boil 8 eggs. When cool enough to handle, remove shells and cut in half lengthwise. Put aside. Prepare batter for frying.

Prepare a sauce with 1½ cups vin rosé, 1 tablespoon white wine vinegar, 1 tablespoon honey, 3 cloves, 1-inch stick cinnamon, ¼ teaspoon salt and a pinch of cayenne. Simmer covered for ½ hour. Just before straining add 2 tablespoons best cognac.

Dip the eggs in the batter and fry in clarified butter (see page 22). Serve with the hot sauce apart.

The sweet-and-sour flavor is quite enticing when one becomes accustomed to it.

Eggs as Prepared in the Creuse

In her Paris apartment on the Left Bank, Miss Toklas serves this dish as a first course, in which case only 1 egg is allowed for each person. If, however, it should be used as an entrée for lunch or supper, one would count on 2 eggs per person.

YOU WILL NEED: Pepper
  Eggs   Cream
  Salt   Swiss cheese

Beat the whites of 8 eggs until very stiff, seasoning them with ½ teaspoon salt and ¼ teaspoon pepper. Place them in the bottom of a well-buttered fireproof dish, flattening the surface with a moist spatula. Make 8 hollows in which you place the yolks of the eggs. Cover each yolk with 1 tablespoon cream. Sprinkle the whites of the eggs with ¾ cup of grated Swiss cheese. Place in 450° oven for 8 minutes and serve piping hot.

Egg Croquettes

Since olive oil is so expensive and rather tricky for deep-fat frying, we suggest that you use Mazola, Wesson or peanut oil instead. Heat to 370° F. If you have an automatically controlled deep-fat fryer or a gas burner with an automatic control, croquettes and all manner of deep-fried foods are practically failproof.

A deep-fat fryer, however, was one modern cooking device which Alice Toklas begged us not to send to her. She knew that with the Paris current the results would be too frustrating. Anyway she is so experienced that she can tell at a glance and a sniff whether the oil is at the right temperature for perfect frying. Here in America the automatic control takes the place of her years of experience.

YOU WILL NEED: *Pepper*
  Butter   *Mace*
  Flour   *Eggs*
  Thin cream   *Olive oil*
  Parsley   *Bread crumbs*
  Salt   *Mushroom sauce*

Make a thick white sauce with 4 tablespoons butter, 3 table-spoons flour and 1½ cups scalded thin cream. Simmer for 15 minutes. Add 1 tablespoon chopped parsley, 1 teaspoon salt, ½ teaspoon pepper, ¼ teaspoon powdered mace and 8 chopped hard-boiled eggs. Cool and shape into thick finger-length rolls. Dip in an egg beaten with 1 tablespoon olive oil and then roll in bread crumbs. Fry in deep olive oil to a golden brown. Drain and serve at once with mushroom sauce (page 100).

Omelette Mancini

This omelette filled with braised sweetbreads is covered with heavy cream and grated cheese. If you like you may whip the cream a little. It makes a fluffier topping. On days when you do not wish to light the oven you could glaze the omelette by placing it at least 5 inches under the electric rotisserie broiler for about 4 or 5 minutes. A 6-egg omelette is usually served to 4 people but because of the rich filling and topping this recipe could serve 5 or even 6.

YOU WILL NEED: *Shallot*
  Eggs   *Pepper*
  Flour   *Lemon juice*
  Salt   *Heavy cream*
  Butter   *Grated cheese, Swiss and*
  Sweetbreads   *Parmesan*

Make an omelette with 6 slightly beaten eggs well mixed with 2 tablespoons flour and a pinch of salt. Melt 3 tablespoons butter in omelette pan and pour in the eggs. After 3 minutes, place on half of it 1 cup diced braised sweetbreads, 1 chopped shallot, ¼ teaspoon salt, ⅛ teaspoon pepper and the juice of ½ lemon. Fold the omelette and place on a buttered fireproof dish. Pour over it 1 cup heavy cream and sprinkle it with ½ cup grated cheese, half Swiss and half Parmesan, and bake in a 350° oven for 10 minutes.

Eggs with Cream and Truffles

Never was a hard-boiled egg (or must we call it a hard-cooked egg?) so dazzlingly glorified. In this recipe Miss Toklas gives directions for dealing with the truffle in its fresh state. Here in the United States, if we are lucky or rich enough to procure truffles, they are in cans, which means that they are already brushed, peeled and cooked. You have only to heat them in Madeira wine and bouillon as Miss Toklas suggests, bringing them very slowly just to a boil (but do not boil). Allow to stand in the hot wine for a few minutes. Then drain, cool and slice. Two or three of the end slices may be finely chopped to make a border.

YOU WILL NEED:

Eggs	Truffles
Whipped cream	Madeira wine
Salt	Bouillon

Boil eggs in water to cover for 12 minutes. Drain and place under running cold water until cool enough to shell. Cover each egg with 3 tablespoons whipped cream into which salt to taste has been stirred.

Allowing ½ truffle per person, brush thoroughly and peel thinly. Chop the peels fine and put aside. Put the truffles in a saucepan with 1 tablespoon Madeira and 1 teaspoon good bouillon per truffle. Cover and cook over lowest flame for 1 hour. Shake the pan from time to time. When the truffles are cooked, drain and cool. Slice thinly and place on the eggs. The chopped peel is for a thin border.

Tender Eggs with Cream and Chives

Actually, these are eggs poached in their shells. You often hear them referred to as "eggs Mollet." It is well worth while to develop the knack of doing them, and it is a knack.

The eggs must be very fresh—if you can get them. Cook the eggs in water that is just moving but not boiling hard, and it must not stop moving. Put in not more than 3 or 4 eggs at a time so as not to lower the temperature too much. Cook scarcely 4 minutes. If the eggs are cooked even a few moments too long, the white has a tendency to cling to the shell. Place immediately under cold water and keep them in cold water so that the shell will come off easily. Crack shell gently and remove as soon as possible.

The lovely lady-poet Louise de Vilmorin is said to have invented this delightful springlike dish.

YOU WILL NEED: Salt
  Eggs   Cayenne
  Whipped cream   Chives

Boil 8 eggs for 4 minutes. Remove from heat, drain and cool under running cold water. Then remove shells carefully, remembering they are tender. Place on serving dish and cover with ¾ cup whipped cream which has been seasoned with ½ teaspoon salt and a pinch of cayenne. Sprinkle with 8 tablespoons slivered chives. Place in refrigerator for 2 hours before serving.

Zucchini Omelette

This dish comes from Italy, where it could be called a frittata. And before that, centuries before, it might have come from China, for the method is so similar. In China, however, and probably here in America, peanut oil would be used instead of *olive oil. And for those of you who use an automatically controlled skillet, the correct temperature is about 385° F.*

YOU WILL NEED:

Young zucchinis	Eggs
Olive oil	Pepper
Salt	Garlic

For 4 persons dice 4 very young zucchinis. Cook them in 3 tablespoons olive oil in skillet over low flame until they are tender and light golden. Add ¼ teaspoon salt. Beat 8 eggs with fork with ½ teaspoon salt and ¼ teaspoon pepper. Pour into hot skillet in which 3 tablespoons olive oil is smoking. Cook the omelette 3 minutes, put the cooked zucchinis on it. Fold over and serve.

It is admissible, indeed it is recommended, to cook the zucchini with garlic.

Eggs à la Tapinade

On the Côte d'Azur on the French Riviera tapinade is made from tiny black olives no bigger than coffee beans . . . the tiniest and tastiest olives in all the world! But it would be a shame to waste such olives on anything but eating plain and straight, even if you could find them, which is very difficult. Any ripe olive would become glamorized when treated in the way Miss Toklas describes.

Incidentally, instead of pounding in a mortar and through a hair sieve you can use the electric blender.

YOU WILL NEED:

Eggs	Capers
Ripe olives	Dry mustard
Boned anchovies	Olive oil
Milk	Mixed spices
Tinned tuna fish	Cognac

This is a Provençal dish. Tapinade is capers.

For 4 people cook 8 eggs for 12 minutes. Then drain and place under running cold water until cool enough to remove shells. Cut in half lengthwise and remove yolks. Put aside while you prepare the sauce tapinade.

Pound in a mortar 1 cup ripe olives—stones naturally removed and the olive meat then measured—½ cup boned anchovies previously soaked in milk, ½ cup tinned tuna fish, 1 cup capers and 1 tablespoon dry mustard. When fine enough pound through a hair sieve. Then slowly add ¾ cup olive oil, 1 tablespoon mixed spices (four spices—see below) and 2 tablespoons good cognac. Mix ¾ of this mixture with the well-crushed yolks of eggs. Fill the hard-boiled whites of eggs with this and then place the rest of the tapinade as a border around the dish.

This sauce keeps well in a covered jar in the refrigerator and is excellent with cold fish.

Four Spices

YOU WILL NEED:
> *Powdered white pepper*
> *⅒ as much powdered cloves*
> *¼ as much powdered ginger*
> *¼ as much powdered nutmeg*

Mix thoroughly. Keep well corked.

CHEESE

Princess Cheese

This is a delightful cinnamon-and-coriander-flavored dessert cheese to serve along with fresh fruit, or, in the Italian manner, with thinly sliced panettone or coffee cake.

YOU WILL NEED:
> Cream cheese
> Salt
> Lemon peel
> Powdered or pounded coriander seed
> Cinnamon
> Sugar

Mix in a bowl ½ pound cream cheese with ⅛ teaspoon salt, 1 grated lemon peel, ⅛ teaspoon powdered or pounded coriander seed, ⅛ teaspoon cinnamon and ⅛ teaspoon sugar. Place in mold lined with waxed paper. Chill in refrigerator for 4 or 5 hours but remove from refrigerator ½ hour before serving.

Purple Cheese

This molded dessert cheese takes on a more definite purple hue if it is made with grape instead of currant jelly. Generally for American tastes the extra tablespoonful of sugar is not needed. The jelly makes it sweet enough to suit our taste.

YOU WILL NEED:
> Cream cheese
> Currant jelly
> Sugar

Mix 1 cup cream cheese, ½ cup currant jelly and 1 tablespoon sugar in electric beater at low speed until perfectly smooth. Then place in a small mold lined with waxed paper and in the refrigerator for 1 hour before serving.

Frozen Cheese Alexandra

This cheese mold is not for dessert but to serve with cocktails or as an accompaniment to salad. It is especially good with fingers of rye bread lightly toasted but not buttered and served very hot as a contrast to the cold, cold cheese.

YOU WILL NEED: *Paprika*
     Butter   *Chives*
     Roquefort cheese   *Sherry*

Mix in blender at lowest speed ½ cup soft butter, 1 cup diced Roquefort cheese, ½ teaspoon paprika, 1 teaspoon chives and ½ cup sherry. When quite smooth remove from blender and place in small molds lined with wax paper. Put in freezing compartment of refrigerator for at least 1 hour before serving. Once removed from molds serve at once.

Cheese Délicieuses

These are fine to serve with cocktails or, if you like, as an accompaniment to a soup or a salad.

YOU WILL NEED: *Nutmeg*
     Egg   *Grated Swiss cheese*
     Salt   *Bread crumbs*
     Pepper   *Peanut oil*

These are delicious and quickly prepared.

For each person allow the beaten white of 1 egg. Season with salt, pepper and nutmeg, fold in 3 tablespoons grated Swiss cheese. Using 2 tablespoons, shape into little sausages and roll in dried bread crumbs. Drop into deep hot peanut oil and fry at 320° F. As soon as they are golden brown, remove with perforated spoon and serve at once.

Fish Court Bouillon

YOU WILL NEED:
> *Fish*
> *White wine*
> *Vegetables as for meat bouillon*

Put in the fish kettle half water and half dry white wine to well cover the fish. Use the same vegetables as for meat court bouillon (see page 40) in quantity proportionate to size of the fish. Be sure the fish is not too delicate to include garlic. Cover the fish kettle and cook the court bouillon for 30 minutes. Remove from heat and when tepid place fish on rack of fish kettle. Bring to heat over medium flame. As soon as it comes to a boil lower heat to least possible flame. It should not boil—scarcely simmer, 12 to 15 minutes will suffice, according to the size of the fish. If the fish is to be eaten cold, remove from flame and allow it to cool in court bouillon.

To Clarify Court Bouillon

YOU WILL NEED:
> *Egg whites and shells*

Strain and discard vegetables and skim off fat. According to the amount of court bouillon add 1 or 2 egg whites to it and also the cracked shells. Bring to a boil, stirring constantly. When it has boiled for 2 minutes, remove and let it stand for 20 minutes without stirring. Then strain through muslin cloth which has been wrung out in cold water.

To Clarify Butter

It is necessary to clarify butter for the preparation of delicate fish, for the frying of chickens and for rissolé potatoes. That has become my specialty since the great Bergerat taught me many years ago.

It is just as easy and as quick to do 2 pounds as to do ½ pound. Cut butter at room temperature in small pieces. Put in a heavy enameled pot over the very lowest possible flame. When the butter has become transparent move the surface about once or twice. On no account must you disturb the residue which will have sunk to the bottom. Let the butter stand for a little while. Then gently ladle the clear top butter into jars. It will keep in a dry cool spot for several months.

French servants like the residue, which they eat with bread. It has a special flavor.

To Fry Fish

Here in the United States, salad or peanut oil would be used instead of olive oil. The method is the same but the temperatures are different. Olive oil is used at about 350° F. At higher temperatures it smokes and breaks. Salad or peanut oil may be safely heated to 360° or 370° F.

YOU WILL NEED:
Fish	Egg yolks
White wine	Bread crumbs
Salt and pepper	Paprika
	Olive oil

Soak the fish in white wine for ½ hour. Dry, salt and pepper, dip in stirred yolks of eggs and then in dry bread crumbs to which have been added paprika and salt. Fry in deep olive oil.

Red Mullets

Mullet is a fish highly regarded in Greece and in France but treated with disdain by many people in the United States. In New York, for instance, it is difficult to find in markets except those of Harlem. If you should find it impossible to get small mullets, porgies may be used.

YOU WILL NEED: Smoked ham
    Red mullets   Olive oil
    Bay leaves   A ravigote or hollandaise sauce

Allow a fish of about 1 pound per person. Do not empty them but remove fins and scales, leaving the heads and tails. Cut parchment paper somewhat larger than the size of a fish and oil the paper generously. Place 1 bay leaf on each paper and on it a fish. Cover with a thin slice of smoked ham. Roll the two ends of the paper securely. Place the enveloped fish in a casserole in which you will have poured 1 tablespoon olive oil per fish. Bake in a 350° oven for about 18 minutes. Turn twice during this time. Serve in their papers. A ravigote or hollandaise sauce (page 108) appropriately accompanies the fish.

Mussels with Saffron

All along the coast of New England tons of mussels go to waste. The same people who pay no attention to them in their own back sea go mad for them in the restaurants of Paris. However, it is a mistake to think that mussels are not available in American cities. Often you can find them in neighborhoods where there are people of Italian descent.

YOU WILL NEED:
    Mussels   Butter
    Shallots   Saffron

Eggs   Heavy cream
Flour   Parsley

Thoroughly wash 2 quarts mussels and place them in a covered
saucepan over high flame with 3 finely chopped shallots and 5
tablespoons butter. Cook until steam escapes. Remove from heat
and drain, keeping the juice they have exuded. Remove the mussels from their shells. Place ½ teaspoon powdered saffron in a
small bowl. Strain the juice through a fine linen cloth into the
bowl and stir until perfectly smooth. Stir the yolks of 3 eggs
with 1 tablespoon flour. Combine with juice and saffron. Place
this mixture over very low heat and stir until spoon is coated.
Add 1 cup heavy cream and the mussels. Heat but do not allow
to boil. Sprinkle 1 tablespoon finely chopped parsley and serve
at once.

Whiting with Wine

*The English and Miss Toklas refer to the fish that we call
whiting in the United States as merlan.*

*In place of whole fresh fish it is possible to use quick-frozen
filets of flounder or perch. Since a filet is entirely edible, ½ to
¾ pound per person should prove adequate.*

YOU WILL NEED: Bread crumbs
    Whiting   Salt and pepper
    Flour   Butter
    Green onions   Tomato paste
    Dry white wine   Anchovies

An excellent, cheap, quick way to prepare a fish.

Allow 1 fish of about 1 pound per person. Wash and dry the
fish. Remove fins, heads and tails. Roll each fish in flour and
place in well-buttered fireproof earthenware dish. For 4 portions
surround by 2 chopped green onions and 1 cup dry white wine.
Cover the fish with dry bread crumbs and dot generously with
butter. Place in 400° oven for 20 minutes, basting twice. Salt and
pepper 5 minutes before serving. Serve very hot.

If ½ cup melted butter into which 2 tablespoons tomato paste have been stirred and 4 finely cut anchovies have been added is poured into the casserole at the last moment, the fish is greatly improved.

Shrimps with Oranges à la James Merril

This is one of the more surprising and least orthodox recipes in Miss Toklas' collection—a conversation dish, to serve perhaps in very small ramekins as a first course for lunch or dinner. Such a good change from the all-too-usual shrimp cocktail! As an appetizer 1 pound of shrimp prepared in this way should make at least 6 servings.

YOU WILL NEED:

Shrimps	Orange juice
Garlic	White wine or pale curaçao
Bay leaf	Butter
Peppercorns	Flour
Onion	Orange peel
Clove	Salt
Dill or fennel	Sugar

Boil 1 pound shrimps 8 minutes in enough water to cover with 1 clove crushed garlic, ½ bay leaf, 6 peppercorns, an onion stuck with a clove and a generous sprig of fresh dill, for which fennel may be substituted. When the shrimps turn pink remove from heat and drain. Shell and de-vein them. Put aside. Prepare a sauce with ½ cup strained shrimp stock, 1 cup orange juice, ½ cup white wine, 2 tablespoons butter, 1½ tablespoons flour, 2 tablespoons finely chopped onion, 2 tablespoons finely chopped orange peel. It will require little salt because of the shrimps. If the oranges are not very sweet add 1 tablespoon sugar. Bring sauce to a boil, simmer for 5 minutes stirring constantly. Add shrimps and, as soon as they are hot, serve.

Pale curaçao can be substituted for the white wine. It will accentuate the orange flavor.

Pike in Half-Mourning

Pike has a great reputation in Paris, Vienna, in China too, but in the United States its renown is confined almost entirely to Jewish gastronomic circles. It is one of the fishes required in most of the classic recipes for gefilte fish.

Canned truffles—the only kind available here—do not need to be cooked but are merely heated in wine.

YOU WILL NEED:	Thyme
Pike	Salt
Red wine	Gelatin
Dry white wine	Truffles
Onions	Sherry, Madeira or champagne
Bay leaf	Eggs
Peppercorns	Mayonnaise
Parsley	Watercress

Prepare this delicious dish at least 12 hours in advance.

For 4 persons wipe but do not wash a 3-pound pike. Remove fins but leave head and tail. Prepare a court bouillon of 3 cups of good red wine, 1 cup good dry white wine, 2 onions, 1 bay leaf, 10 peppercorns, several stalks of parsley, a small twig of thyme and 1 tablespoon salt. Simmer for ½ hour. Remove from heat and when tepid place the fish on the rack of the fish kettle. Cover and bring to the boil over high flame. As soon as it boils remove from heat. Allow the fish to cool covered in the court bouillon—the best way to cook a fish. When cold drain the fish and place on serving dish. Strain the court bouillon through a linen cloth. Soak 2 ounces gelatin in ½ cup water. In 5 minutes add to reheated court bouillon. While this is cooling prepare the decorations for the fish.

Cook 2 fine truffles for ¼ hour in sherry or Madeira or—better still—in champagne. Slice the truffles when cold. Remove yolks from 4 hard-boiled eggs, replace with sliced truffles. Pound yolks of eggs or crush them with a fork. When the court bouillon commences to stiffen add to half of it 1 cup green mayonnaise, that is, ¾ cup ordinary mayonnaise to which ¼ cup pounded and strained parsley and watercress has been added. Cover the fish, except the head, with the green mayonnaise. Imbed in it the whites of eggs with the truffles and sprinkle the crushed yolks of eggs according to your taste. Cover with the rest of the gelatin. Serve cold but not frozen.

Blue Trout

YOU WILL NEED:

Trout	Onion
Vinegar	Celery
Dry white wine	Peppercorns
Carrot	Salt
	Green hollandaise sauce

Trout can become blue; they do when prepared in this way. But you must procure very fresh fish and they must not have been washed nor must the scales have been removed. Allow at least a ½-pound fish per person. As soon as possible after they have been caught throw them into a kettle of fast-boiling vinegar. The moment the vinegar reboils remove the fish and place them at once in a hot but not boiling court bouillon which has been prepared in advance: 1 bottle good dry white wine, 2 cups water, 1 diced carrot, 1 diced onion, 2 stalks celery, 6 peppercorns and 1 tablespoon salt—which has been simmered, covered, for 1 hour, strained and brought to the boil again. Place the fish on the rack of the kettle and steam, covered, for 15 minutes. Cool over the court bouillon. Serve with a green hollandaise sauce (see page 114). You will have a success with the blue fish and the green sauce.

Truites en Chemise

This is, without a doubt, one of the most interesting and attractive fish dishes that I have ever encountered. Our first in-

troduction came through Alice Toklas, who took us to lunch one day at Gaffner's, a modest restaurant near her apartment— modest but with a reputation resplendent amongst epicures all over the world.

The trout arrived wrapped in the thinnest sheath of a crêpe so crisp and tender that it offered no more resistance to the fork than the delicate fish beneath.

Fine as it is at Gaffner's, Miss Toklas says that truites en chemise is in reality the specialty of a railroad-station café— the Relais Gastronomique at the Gare de l'Est in Paris—and it is from them that she has this recipe.

YOU WILL NEED:	Light cream
Mushrooms	Eggs
Butter	Cognac
Salt	Milk
Pepper	Trout
Flour	Lemon juice

Sauté ½ pound finely chopped mushrooms in 3 tablespoons butter. Salt and pepper to taste. Add a little flour. Stir in ½ cup light cream. Cook until lightly thickened. Keep warm.

To prepare the crêpes, mix in an electric beater at low speed 1 cup less 1 tablespoon flour with 3 eggs, one at a time. When there are no lumps add 2 tablespoons cognac, ½ teaspoon salt and 2 tablespoons melted butter. Gradually stir in 1½ cups milk. Let the batter rest for a couple of hours.

Bake the crêpes in a 6-inch pan, well buttered, over a fairly brisk heat. Pour a little of the batter into the pan and tip so that it runs all over the surface. Turn with a spatula and cook the other side.

During this time prepare the trout. Dip 6 trout in flour, salt and pepper, and sauté in butter. When just cooked through remove from pan.

Place a little of the mushroom mixture on each crêpe. Roll a trout in each crêpe with the head and tail sticking out. Place on lighted chafing dish with a little butter and lemon juice. Serve piping hot.

Godiveau Lyonnaise, or Quenelles

When she was introduced to the marvels of the blender, Miss Toklas wrote an article in House Beautiful entitled "A Blessed Blender in the Home."

"Let us commence," she wrote, "with the right way to make one of France's greatest dishes, the delicate morsels of forcemeat of fish called quenelles."

These quenelles are one of the gastronomic triumphs of the Burgundy wine country and generally they carry the name of the city of Lyon, known as the gastronomic capital of France and, by inference, the world.

Use perch if you can't get pike.

YOU WILL NEED:	Beef-kidney fat
Eggs	Pike
Flour	Salt
Butter	Pepper
Milk	Nutmeg

Place in the blender the yolks of 3 eggs with ⅔ cup flour, 4 tablespoons melted butter. Blend 1 minute and while blender is still running add ⅔ cup hot milk. Keep blending until perfectly smooth, place in a small saucepan over medium heat and cook about 6 minutes, stirring constantly. Put aside to cool. This mixture is called panada.

Place in the bottom of the blender the whites of 2 eggs, then add ½ pound fat from beef kidney, skin removed and cut into small cubes. When perfectly smooth remove from the blender with a rubber spatula and replace with ½ pound cubed pike (weighed after bones and skin have been removed). Add ½ teaspoon salt, ¼ teaspoon pepper, ¼ teaspoon nutmeg; in about 3 minutes add the panada, fat and egg mixture. Blend first at low speed, then at high speed until perfectly smooth and very fine.

The mixture is now ready to be rolled between floured hands

into finger lengths and poached for 5 minutes in salted water,
1 teaspoon to the quart. Be careful the quenelles do not stick
to the bottom of the pan or together. Remove from water with
perforated spoon and place on a kitchen towel to dry; pat them
quite dry. They are now ready to be simmered for 10 minutes in
whatever sauce is to be served with them. They may be served
around a boiled fish in a cream sauce or in the juice of a braised
chicken or around a roast veal, or they may be served by them-
selves as an entrée. In which case the sky is the limit for the
sauce you choose, providing your choice is a delicate one. One
which can be recommended is:

Sauce Royale

YOU WILL NEED: *Green onions*
    Chicken bouillon   *Truffles*
    Butter   *Heavy cream*
    Flour   *Dry sherry*

Prepare a chicken velouté: Warm 4 cups of chicken bouillon;
place 1 cup in the blender along with 4 tablespoons softened
butter, 4 tablespoons flour; blend till perfectly smooth. Add 3
green onions cut into pieces and blend a few seconds, just long
enough to chop the onions. Add the sauce in the blender to the
rest of the heated bouillon and simmer 1 hour, stirring occasionally to prevent scorching.

Meanwhile place 6 tablespoons truffles (3-ounce tin) along
with ¼ cup chicken bouillon into the blender and blend until
the particles practically disappear.

At the end of the simmering add to the sauce ½ cup heavy
cream. Then strain, replace over heat and stir in the truffles
from the blender. When the sauce boils, carefully add the
quenelles. Cover and simmer gently for 10 minutes. Then add
⅓ cup butter, cut in small pieces, and 2 tablespoons good, dry
sherry. Do not allow the sauce to boil; do not stir, but gently
tip the saucepan in all directions. When the butter is melted
and the sherry is amalgamated, serve.

Salmon Soufflé

Some people might prefer to call this a mousse rather than a soufflé. It is moist, fine textured rather than puffy, and unbrowned.

YOU WILL NEED:

Eggs	Pepper
Raw salmon	Heavy cream
Salt	Shrimp sauce

This is another one of France's gastronomic achievements.

Place in the bottom of the blender the whites of two eggs, then 1⅓ cups cubed raw salmon measured after bones, skin and fat have been removed. Add ½ teaspoon salt, ⅛ teaspoon pepper, blend at low speed until fish and eggs form a smooth paste. Then turn to high speed and blend until the particles are very fine. Place in bowl surrounded with cracked ice. Do not place in refrigerator; it has not the same effect.

Beat, not too stiff, two cups of heavy cream and add it to the fish and white-of-egg mixture surrounded by ice. Beat the whites of 4 eggs very stiff but not dry, and gently fold them into the mixture, which you will now remove from ice and pour into a buttered soufflé dish sufficiently deep to permit the soufflé to rise. Stand in a pan of hot but not boiling water and bake in a moderate (350° F.) oven for about 40 minutes. Remove the soufflé gently from the dish and serve surrounded with shrimp sauce. Recipe follows.

Shrimp Sauce

To make this sauce, de-veined quick-frozen jumbo shrimp in their shells may be used instead of green or fresh shrimp. Bottled clam juice may be substituted for fish fumet or stock.

Regular salt will do, but sea salt, which you can buy from health-food shops, has more flavor because it is less refined.

YOU WILL NEED:
Flour
Fish fumet or stock   *Heavy cream*
Butter   *Jumbo shrimp*

Make 4 cups of fish fumet or stock, using 1 pound of heads, tails and fins. Your fishman, if he is amiable, will give them to you. If he is not, buy ½ pound of whiting, hake or fresh cod. Cover with 4 cups cold water, ½ cup dry white wine, add 1 sliced carrot, 1 sliced leek, 1 sliced onion and 5 whole peppercorns, a bouquet of parsley, ½ bay leaf, a sprig of thyme, 1 clove garlic, a few grains freshly grated nutmeg. Add ½ teaspoon sea salt. Cover and cook slowly for 2 hours.

Make a blond roux by adding to 3 tablespoons melted butter ¼ cup flour. When perfectly smooth slowly add all but 1 cup of the strained fish fumet. Cook slowly 20 minutes, skimming any fat that may rise to the surface. Add 5 tablespoons heavy cream and cook uncovered until the sauce is reduced by one quarter.

During this time, boil, shell and remove the black vein from ¾ pound jumbo shrimp. Place in the blender 1 cup of the fish stock and the shells and heads of the shrimp with 5 tablespoons softened butter and 4 or 5 of the smaller shrimp. Blend until perfectly smooth and very fine. Add to the sauce, heat the shelled shrimps in the sauce and pour around your soufflé.

(Another way to make a good shrimp sauce very quickly: Use 1 can quick-frozen cream-of-shrimp soup. Add ¼ soup can of milk or water and ¼ soup can filled with white wine, ½ clove garlic put through the press and a little freshly grated nutmeg. This makes 2 cups of sauce. —P.C.)

Parmesan Bavarois

Essentially this is a Bavarian cream, but it is not sweetened and it is not a dessert but rather a cold entrée to be served as a first course at a summer luncheon or dinner or as a main dish for luncheon or a buffet supper. In France it might be spooned directly from its own glass bowl or terrine. American hostesses may prefer to mold it, in a ring perhaps, and garnish with hearts of lettuce or romaine.

In Haiti I have tasted such a dish presented as a crown on a platter ringed with "flowers" that had been cut out of sweet red peppers.

YOU WILL NEED: *Gelatin*
  Milk   *Grated Parmesan cheese*
  Eggs   *Heavy cream*

For 4 people put 1 cup milk in a saucepan over medium heat. When it is about to boil pour over the well-stirred yolks of 4 eggs. Replace over low heat and stir until the spoon is coated. Remove from heat and stir occasionally. Melt ⅓ tablespoon gelatin in ¼ cup hot milk and add to milk-and-egg mixture. Stir carefully until the gelatin is dissolved. Then add ¼ cup finely grated Parmesan cheese. When cold fold in ¾ cup whipped heavy cream. Place in refrigerator for 1 hour.

Your Own Noodles with Buttered Crumbs

YOU WILL NEED:
  Flour   *Eggs*
  Salt   *Butter*
  Nutmeg   *Bread crumbs*

33

Sift 2 cups flour, 1 teaspoon salt and a pinch of nutmeg. Add the yolks of five eggs and 1 whole egg. Mix thoroughly with a fork and then knead on a floured board. Roll into a ball and put aside for several hours. Divide into three parts and roll each on a lightly floured board to paper thinness. Dry for ½ hour, roll up and cut in strips ¼ inch wide. Bring 1 quart water with 1 teaspoon salt to rolling boil. Drop the noodles in the saucepan, a few at a time. The water must not cease to boil. Stir gently with a fork and reduce to low boil. Boil for 10 minutes. Remove from flame and drain. Cover—while the buttered crumbs are prepared.

Place ½ pound butter in small saucepan over low heat. As soon as the butter is golden brown add to it 4 tablespoons dried bread crumbs. When the butter has reboiled, pour over drained noodles and serve at once. Delicious.

Vegetable Cornets

Despite her lightly veiled disdain of deep-freeze vegetables, I have a feeling that Miss Toklas would approve of frozen artichoke hearts. They are very convenient to use in this recipe.

YOU WILL NEED:

Green peas	Artichokes
String beans	Ham
Small carrots	Clarified chicken-broth jelly
New potatoes	Gelatin
Tips of green asparagus	Basil
Mushrooms	Chives

This is a suitable entrée for a spring lunch or a simple dinner. If deep-freeze vegetables, which I do not use, are acceptable to you, it can be considered a possible dish for any season of the year. The spring vegetables, green peas, tender young string beans, small carrots, new potatoes, tips of green asparagus, mushrooms and hearts of young artichokes, must all be cooked separately and not overcooked. To cook them separately, tie in little bags of parchment paper, cook in a large saucepan of boiling water.

If the vegetables are really young and small it will not be necessary to cut any of them—with the possible exception of artichokes. For 8 cornets, 6 cups of vegetables are required. Divide the 6 cups of cooked vegetables into 8 portions and place on 8 slices of ham, fat and skin removed. Roll and place the cornets side by side in a well-buttered deep dish. Cover with 4 cups clarified chicken-broth jelly in which 2 tablespoons gelatin have been dissolved. Chill, sprinkle with chopped basil and minced chives.

Nymph Aurora

The romantic name of nymph refers to shrimp as well as water plants and sea sprites. This is a dish that deserves a romantic setting. You could if you liked serve it inside a ring of rice. But why not be Parisian and serve it as a first course accompanied only by crusty bread or rolls and chilled white wine!

YOU WILL NEED:

Chicken bouillon	Salt
Onions	Lemon juice
Bay leaf	Cornstarch
Marjoram	Shrimps
Peppercorns	Green coloring
Mace	Heavy cream

Cook for 12 minutes 1 quart chicken bouillon with 2 sliced onions, ½ bay leaf, 1 sprig marjoram, 6 peppercorns, 1 blade of mace, ½ teaspoon salt, 2 tablespoons lemon juice and 2 tablespoons cornstarch well mixed with 2 tablespoons water. Remove from heat and strain. Then add 2 cups boiled, shelled and deveined shrimps. Add enough green coloring to lightly tint. Heat the shrimps in strained sauce. At the last moment beat in ½ cup whipped heavy cream and serve at once.

A Common but Novel Entrée

You might describe this dish as a corn-and-shrimp omelette or a frittata or a corn-and-shrimp version of the Chinese eggs foo-yung. No matter, it is very good, very quick, simple and delicious. The recipe makes servings for 4.

YOU WILL NEED:

No. 2 tin sweet corn	*Eggs*
Flour	*Shrimps*
Salt and pepper	*Salad oil*

Drain 1 No. 2 tin sweet corn, putting aside 3 tablespoons of it. Mix with the drained corn 3 tablespoons flour, adding salt and pepper to taste, 2 well-beaten eggs and 1 cup cooked, shelled and de-veined shrimps. Heat 3 tablespoons salad oil in hot skillet. When it is very hot pour in the mixture and cook for 3 minutes. Fold with the aid of a spatula and serve at once.

Ham and Oyster Pie

You could use a biscuit-mix topping. In that case, in order to get the butter taste, brush the pie with a little melted butter before putting it in the oven. Do this not only for the taste but for the beautiful golden glow that the butter imparts. This recipe makes a big pie, almost 2 quarts of filling, so you should use a 3-quart casserole. Makes 6 to 8 servings.

YOU WILL NEED:

Ham	*Marjoram*
Oysters	*Thin cream*
Green peas	*Butter*
Flour	*Flour*
Salt	*Baking powder*
Pepper	*Pastry leaves*

Dice 2 cups boiled ham, add 1 pint oysters and 2 cups cooked green peas.

Make a pale roux of 1½ tablespoons butter, 1 tablespoon flour, 1 teaspoon salt and ½ teaspoon powdered pepper, a pinch of marjoram. Cook till lightly colored. Add 1 cup thin cream, stir constantly and simmer for 10 minutes. Mix with ham, oysters and peas. Butter a fireproof deep dish. Prepare a biscuit dough of 3 tablespoons butter, 2 cups sifted flour, 2½ teaspoons baking powder and ½ cup cold water. Roll out ⅔ of the dough and place in the bottom and sides of the dish. Pour in the mixture. Roll out the rest of the dough and cover the mixture. Pinch the sides together. Cut out a vent in the center and surround with some pastry leaves.

Bake 30 minutes in a preheated 350° oven and serve at once.

Ham Fritters

Miss Toklas explains, "This is a misnomer, for fritters are small and fried, and this is large and baked, which of course does not affect its excellence as an entrée."

Lovely to serve with broiled tomatoes and lightly cooked leaf spinach, the recipe makes 4 to 6 servings.

YOU WILL NEED: Heavy cream
   Soft butter   Grated Parmesan cheese
   Eggs   Ham

Gradually add 4½ tablespoons soft butter to the stirred yolks of 4 eggs. Slowly stir in ½ cup heavy cream, 2 tablespoons grated Parmesan cheese and ½ cup diced ham. Spread on a buttered shallow baking dish about 9" x 14" and place in a preheated 350° oven for 5 minutes. Remove from oven and quickly brush with ½ cup heavy cream and sprinkle with ½ cup chopped ham. Return to oven and bake 15 minutes further.

Sausages in Wine

Quick-frozen brown 'n' serve sausages may be used instead of uncooked sausages, in which case you have only to brown them, then place in the casserole with mushrooms, white wine and cream as directed. A pound of sausages prepared in this manner will serve 3.

YOU WILL NEED:

Small pork sausages   Dry white wine

Mushrooms   Cream

Put 1 pound small pork sausages in dry skillet over low flame. When cooked on all sides remove from heat and drain. Place in casserole with ½ cup mushrooms, ½ cup dry white wine and ¼ cup cream. Cover and place in 300° oven for 25 minutes.

Sweetbreads à la Lyonnaise

When Miss Toklas calls for a sweetbread as she does in this recipe she means a pair of sweetbreads. In that case a recipe like this will serve 2 generously.

YOU WILL NEED:

Sweetbread   Cloves

Fat salt pork   Tarragon leaves

Butter   Bouillon

Parsley   Dry white wine

Garlic   Flour

Green onion   Eggs

Soak a sweetbread in cold water for 1 hour. Rinse and place in covered saucepan covered with cold water. Boil for ¼ hour. Drain and rinse in cold water. Remove fat, skin and tubes. Cut ½ pound fat salt pork, skin removed, in strips suitable for larding the sweetbread, and place in boiling water for a moment. Place them one by one in larding needle and run them through the sweetbread. They should extend well beyond each end. Place the sweetbread in saucepan with 2 tablespoons butter, several sprigs parsley, 1 clove garlic crushed, 1 green onion, 2 cloves, several tarragon leaves and 1 cup good bouillon. Cook over medium flame for ½ hour. Then remove sweetbread, strain and skim sauce. Replace sauce over flame and reduce until it is almost a glaze. Scrape to detach the glaze adhering to bottom and sides of pan. Add to this 2 tablespoons butter, 2 tablespoons dry white wine and 1 teaspoon flour. Stir and simmer. When the juice in the pan is perfectly smooth remove from heat; add the well-stirred yolks of 2 eggs. Replace sweetbread in sauce. Heat but on no account boil. Serve hot.

Sweetbread and Artichoke Stew

If in this recipe frozen artichoke hearts are used, they are cut in 2 rather than 4 parts. Or if you wish, you need not cut them at all, since they are quite small.

YOU WILL NEED:

Sweetbread	Basil leaves
Artichokes	Clove
Green onion	White wine
Garlic	Broth (veal)
Parsley	Butter
Bay leaf	Flour

Soak a sweetbread in salted cold water for 1 hour. Put in saucepan of cold water; bring to a boil. Remove sweetbread and drain; rinse under running cold water. Remove skin and tubes. Boil for ¼ hour. Drain, cut into large cubes and put aside.

Wash 4 artichokes thoroughly, cut the hearts in 4 pieces each and boil about 20 minutes in salted water.

Boil a green onion, 1 clove garlic, several parsley stalks, 1 bay leaf, several basil leaves and 1 clove in ¾ cup white wine and ¼ cup veal broth. Strain. Mix 1½ tablespoons butter and 1 tablespoon flour, thicken the sauce with this. Boil for 20 minutes. If the juice is too thick add a bit of white wine. Mix sweetbreads with artichokes in sauce and serve hot.

MEATS

Court Bouillon—for Meat

YOU WILL NEED:

Meat	Carrots
Salt	Shallots
Whole peppers	Leeks
½ veal knuckle	Bay leaf
Nutmeg	Parsley
Coriander seeds	Celery
Cloves	Garlic
Onion	Thyme
	Basil

Put enough water into the pot to well cover the meat that is to be cooked. Bring uncovered to a quick boil. Be prepared with a perforated spoon as soon as any scum arises. Lower heat at once. Continue to skim until no more scum arises. Add salt, whole peppers, ½ veal knuckle, a piece of whole nutmeg, a few coriander seeds, 2 cloves stuck in an onion, 2 carrots, 2 shallots, 2 leeks, bay leaf, a bunch of parsley stalks, 2 celery stalks, a clove of garlic and a sprig of thyme and basil. Cover and simmer for 4 or 5 hours. Strain.

Beefsteak in the Polish Manner

This recipe is reminiscent of the rouladen of Vienna. The sauce will remind you of the Russian beef Stroganoff. Julienne potato sticks seem particularly appropriate as an accompaniment and you can get very good ones in tins. They are at their best when warmed in a moderate oven for about 3 minutes.

YOU WILL NEED: *Shallots*
  Filet of beef   *Beef bouillon*
  Anchovies   *Heavy cream*
  Parsley   *Paprika*

Have your butcher cut as thinly as possible as many slices of filet as you will require. I allow 2 slices per person. Salt each slice and add per slice 1 crushed anchovy, 1 teaspoon finely chopped parsley and 1 teaspoon finely minced shallots. Simmer in Dutch oven over lowest heat with ½ cup beef bouillon and ½ cup heavy cream. Baste frequently. It will require another ½ cup beef bouillon and another ½ cup heavy cream, gradually added as needed. Be careful that the meat does not stick to the bottom of the pot. Between bastings shake the pot. The sauce should be unctuous and there should be sufficient to cover the meat. A quarter of an hour before serving add 1 tablespoon paprika for 8 slices of meat. It will take about 1¼ hours to cook.

Beefsteak with Shallots

First grill your favorite type of steak in your favorite way and then proceed to bedizen it with shallots.

"Shallots," Miss Toklas says, "are like garlic. You do or you do not like them."

Actually they taste like little red onions with garlicky overtones. They are distressingly difficult to find in the United States except in the larger cities or in the foreign sections of smaller towns. If you must you can order them by mail. In a dry airy place they will keep well for at least a couple of months.

YOU WILL NEED: *Butter*
  Shallots   *Salt*
  Beefsteak   *Pepper*

For 4 persons take 1 pound peeled shallots. Place over low heat in a covered saucepan with ¼ cup water. When they can be pierced with a knife, in about 20 minutes, remove them from heat, drain thoroughly and place in a heated serving dish and place on them the grilled beefsteak. Pour over ⅓ cup melted butter. Sprinkle with salt and pepper and serve at once.

Marjoram Jokany

Cutting the meat into strips and presenting it with a rich, winy, creamy sauce makes a little go a long way. A mere 2 pounds of beef can make 6 servings, especially when presented with wheat pilaff, kasha, rice or fine noodles. A green salad or a tomato aspic would go well with it, the aspic topped not with a rich mayonnaise, which would be too much, but only a small spoonful of sour cream.

YOU WILL NEED:

Filet of beef	Garlic
Onions	Fat salt pork
Butter	Marjoram
Salt	Dry white wine
	Heavy cream

Cut 2 pounds filet of beef in thin slices and then in narrow strips as for a boeuf Stroganoff. Brown lightly 4 chopped onions in a Dutch oven in 3 tablespoons butter. Then add the meat, ½ teaspoon salt, 1 clove crushed garlic, ½ pound fat salt pork without rind cut in ½-inch cubes, 1 teaspoon powdered marjoram and ¾ cup dry white wine. Cover and cook gently for ¾ of an hour, stirring from time to time. Add 2 cups heavy cream, heat thoroughly but do not allow to boil. Serve very hot.

Christmas Estoufat

YOU WILL NEED:

Salty fat pork	Carrots
Salt	Buttocks of beef
Pepper	(round steak or pot roast)
Onions	Brandy
	Red wine

This is a dish served in Provence for the traditional supper after the midnight mass of Christmas Eve. There is a special earthenware dish for cooking meat slowly of which the potters along the Mediterranean coast make a specialty. The cover holds about 1½ cups water to prevent the evaporation of the juices in the pot, like the covers of our Dutch ovens but deeper. In this daubière is placed 1½ pounds salty fat pork with its rind. It is this rind which will give the sauce its consistency. Then add 1 tablespoon salt and 1 teaspoon pepper, 2 large onions cut in quarters, 2 large carrots and 6 pounds of the under side of the buttocks of beef. Pour over the meat ¾ cup good brandy and enough good dry red wine to cover the meat abundantly. Over the top of the meat place a piece of heavy parchment paper and tie securely to the daubière. Cover and fill the hollow rim with hot water which must be renewed as soon as it is dry. Place the daubière in a warm oven, reduce at once to lowest heat. Leave in the oven for 24 hours. Do not be tempted for an instant to remove the parchment paper, just shake the daubière from time to time and add water to the cover as needed. Before going to mass the farmer's wife uncovers the daubière for the first time to skim the fat from the sauce so that upon their return from mass she will have nothing more to do than to remove the skin from the salt pork and cut the fat into small pieces.

Of course one does not have to wait for Christmas to prepare or to enjoy this excellent dish nor is one limited to beef for cooking an estoufat. I have made it successfully with mutton. Also with a monstrously large hen.

Veal Chops en Papillote

YOU WILL NEED:

Veal chops	Anchovy filets
Parsley	Garlic
Mushrooms	Salt
Shallots	Pepper
Onions	Butter

For 4 veal chops—do not remove bones—chop 4 tablespoons parsley, 4 tablespoons raw mushrooms, 1 tablespoon shallots, 1 tablespoon onions, 4 anchovy filets and 1 crushed clove of garlic. Add 1 teaspoon salt, ¼ teaspoon pepper and 1 table-spoon butter. Cut heavy waxed paper the shape of the cutlets, doubling the straight bone side and large enough to securely roll around the other three sides. Brush the paper liberally with butter. Place a cutlet on a papillote and on the cutlet ¼ of the chopped mixture. Roll securely around the 3 sides and place the 4 papillotes in a Dutch oven over low heat and cover. Shake the pot frequently so that the paper does not stick to the bottom of the pot. Turn the papillotes 2 or 3 times while they are cooking for about ¾ of an hour. Serve in their wrappings.

Cold Veal Garnished with Artichokes and Green Asparagus Tips

Once again frozen artichokes and asparagus tips may be used instead of fresh vegetables.

YOU WILL NEED:

Veal cutlets	Pepper
Butter	Heavy cream
Port wine	Hearts of artichokes
Salt	Tips of green asparagus

For 4 people place 4 slices of veal cutlet in 3 tablespoons melted butter in Dutch oven over low flame. Cover and shake the pot. In 20 minutes, when the meat will have exuded some of its juice, pour over it ½ cup of an excellent dry port wine, ¾ teaspoon salt and ¼ teaspoon pepper. Turn the cutlets, add ¾ cup heavy cream and cover the pot. Simmer for 20 minutes more. Remove from pot and place on serving dish with the cutlets overlapping. Pour the sauce over them. Serve cool, not chilled. Place alternately around the meat boiled hearts of artichokes and small bunches of boiled tips of green asparagus. The vegetables will need no seasoning but salt; the sauce will give all the flavoring the dish requires.

A very good hot-weather dish.

Veal Bitik with Lemon

This amount will make 8 small croquettes. Especially with the cream sauce, 2 should be an ample serving for each person. No starch is necessary—only a green vegetable or a salad.

YOU WILL NEED:

Lean veal	Mace
Dried bread crumbs	Basil
Milk	Butter
Salt	Beef bouillon
Pepper	Lemon
	Heavy cream

Grind 1 pound lean veal twice. Cover 1 cup dried bread crumbs with hot milk. Remove bread crumbs when tepid and squeeze dry. Place with chopped veal in bowl and add ½ teaspoon salt, ¼ teaspoon pepper, ¼ teaspoon mace, ½ teaspoon basil. Pat into croquettes 1 inch thick. Melt 4 tablespoons butter in a skillet and gently cook croquettes over low flame until they are browned on both sides. Remove to heated serving dish and keep hot. Pour ¾ cup good beef bouillon and juice of 1 lemon into skillet. Detach any glaze that is at the bottom and sides of skillet. When well mixed boil 1 minute and add 2 cups heavy cream. Heat but do not boil. Pour over croquettes. Place 1 slice lemon on each croquette and serve.

Empanadas de Carne

Meat-filled turnovers with raisins and olives are characteristic of Spain. Probably they derive from the Near East and are found in South America, in Mexico and the West Indies.

These may be served as a first course or an entrée for luncheon. But their most popular role in the modern American menu is that of a cocktail snack.

This recipe makes about 4 large turnovers or could be cut into 4 dozen cocktail-size empanadas.

YOU WILL NEED:

Veal and pork	Eggs
Onions	Seedless raisins
Butter	Stuffed olives
Powdered sweet Spanish	Flour
pepper	Baking powder
Salt	Lard

Grind very fine 1½ cups raw meat—veal and pork is a good combination—with 2 small onions. Brown in 2 tablespoons butter, add ½ teaspoon powdered sweet Spanish pepper, ½ teaspoon salt, 1 sliced hard-boiled egg, 3 tablespoons seedless raisins and 3 sliced stuffed olives. Prepare a dough of 2 cups sifted flour and 4 teaspoons baking powder, ⅛ cup lard and ⅛ cup butter and ¼ cup water. Divide the dough into 4 balls. Roll each one into a thin square. Place ¼ of the chopped mixture on each square. Fold the dough over and pinch the edges securely. Place on buttered baking sheet, brush with yolk of egg diluted with 1 teaspoon water and bake in 375° oven for 20 minutes. Serve at once.

Veal with a Sauce as Green as a Field

YOU WILL NEED:

Veal	Bay leaf
Butter	Thyme
Flour	Parsley
Chicken or veal bouillon	Green onion
Dry white wine	Garlic
	Salt

Pepper   Croutons, puff-paste cres-
Spinach   cents or noodles
Eggs   Bread crumbs

Allow for 4 people 2½ pounds veal after the bones are removed. Cut in pieces about 2-inch cubes. Melt 3 tablespoons
butter in Dutch oven over low heat and place in it the pieces
of meat. Stir with a wooden spoon until the pieces are covered
with butter but without browning them. Then add 1½ tablespoons flour. Continue to stir. Add ½ cup chicken or veal bouillon and ½ cup good dry white wine and a bouquet of ½ bay
leaf, a sprig of thyme, 3 stalks parsley, 1 green onion and a clove
of garlic. Cook over medium heat for ¾ hour, turning the meat
frequently. Add 1 teaspoon salt and ½ teaspoon pepper. Cook 1
pound spinach, that has been carefully washed, for 7 minutes
over low flame. Drain and place under running cold water.
Press out all water and pound through a hair sieve. Remove
bouquet from Dutch oven and place strained spinach in the
juice. Stir the yolks of 3 eggs in a bowl, slowly add some of the
juice. Add to the sauce, stirring until the spoon is coated. Do not
allow to boil. Serve hot.

The meat may be surrounded by fried croutons (see below)
or puff-paste crescents (see page 142) or noodles with browned
bread crumbs (see page 33).

Fried Croutons

YOU WILL NEED:
    Bread
    Butter

Cut bread (crusts removed) into cubes and fry in deep butter
in skillet over low flame or in oven with door open. Toss frequently. Should be golden brown.

Veal in the Manner of the Beauce

This recipe should provide 6 servings.

YOU WILL NEED:

Filet of veal	*Pepper*
Bouillon	*Béchamel sauce*
Salt	*Dried bread crumbs*

Roast a 2½-pound filet of veal in a 350° oven for 1¼ hours, basting every 5 minutes with 1 cup bouillon in which 1 tablespoon salt and ½ teaspoon pepper have been dissolved. When roasted remove from oven. When cold cut in thin slices and cover them with half of a thick béchamel sauce (see page 97) made of 2 tablespoons butter, 2 tablespoons flour, 1½ cups bouillon to which has been added ½ cup grated Swiss cheese. Reconstruct the filet by placing the slices on top of each other and pressing them down. Roll the reconstructed filet in the rest of the béchamel sauce and sprinkle the top and sides liberally with dried bread crumbs. Place in fireproof serving dish and then in a 450° oven for 10 minutes. During this time skim the juice in the roasting pan and pour around the veal.

Stuffed Breast of Veal

YOU WILL NEED:

Breast of veal	*Pepper*
Onions	*Butter*
Bread	*Egg*
Milk	*Paprika*
Calf's liver	*Veal bouillon*
Beef fat from kidneys	*Mushrooms*
Salt	*Heavy cream*

This is not, as will be observed at a glance, ordinary stuffed veal.

Cook for 10 minutes in as little water as possible ½ cup

chopped onions. Drain and put aside. Soak 1 cup crumbled bread, crusts removed, in hot milk to cover. Squeeze dry and put aside. Place in blender at low speed ½ pound of calf's liver from which tubes and nerves have been removed before weighing and ¼ pound beef fat from the kidneys. This should be cubed. When perfectly smooth add the soaked bread, the onions, ½ teaspoon salt and ¼ teaspoon pepper. Blend 2 to 4 minutes longer. Heat 4 tablespoons butter in a pan and, when it bubbles, add the mixture. When it commences to brown, remove from heat, add 1 egg and mix.

Place on table the breast of veal from which you have had your butcher remove the bones, open out and flatten. Spread the stuffing evenly on it, leaving a small margin on all sides. Roll the breast and tie it so that none of the stuffing will escape but not too tight because it will expand in the heat of cooking. Put 4 tablespoons butter in an iron pot. When it bubbles reduce heat and place meat in the pot. Lightly brown on all sides. Then add ½ teaspoon salt and ½ teaspoon paprika. Cover the pot and simmer for 2 hours. If it is necessary while the meat is cooking, add ½ cup veal bouillon. After 2 hours add 1 pound thinly sliced mushrooms and any bit of stuffing that may have remained over. Cover the pot and cook further for 15 minutes. Then add ½ cup heavy cream; do not allow to boil, do not stir, but tip the pot in all directions. Remove from pot, place on serving dish after strings have been removed, pour the sauce and mushrooms around the meat; serve hot.

Meat Loaf in My Fashion

YOU WILL NEED:

Bread	Onion
White wine	Shallot
Calf's liver	Garlic
Lean veal	Mushrooms
Lean pork	Celery salt

Pepper   Powdered thyme
Mace   Powdered basil
Dry mustard   Eggs
Orange   Butter
Powdered bay leaf Beef bouillon

This is more like a pâté than the usual meat loaf. It is exceedingly fine and smooth in texture.

Place in a bowl 1 cup bread which has been soaked in white wine to cover and then squeezed dry, ½ pound cubed calf's liver, ½ pound cubed lean veal, 1 cup cubed lean pork, 1 diced onion, 2 shallots, 1 clove garlic, ½ pound cubed raw mushrooms, 1 teaspoon celery salt, 1 teaspoon pepper, ¼ teaspoon mace, 1 teaspoon dry mustard, the zest of ½ of a medium-sized orange, ¼ teaspoon powdered bay leaf, ¼ teaspoon powdered thyme, ½ teaspoon powdered basil. Place in blender 1 or 2 cupfuls at a time. To the last batch, after it is quite smooth, add 2 eggs and blend another minute or two. Mix everything together well in the bowl.

Butter very generously a fireproof earthenware dish; place the mixture in it, forming into a loaf with a knife frequently dipped into melted butter. Then spread over it 6 tablespoons melted butter, covering the sides as well as the top. Bake in 450° F. oven. After ¼ hour pour into the dish around the loaf ½ cup dry white wine and 1 cup beef bouillon. Baste every ¼ hour. After the meat has been in the oven ¾ hour, remove. It can now be served at it is or served cold, but it is delicious covered with mashed potatoes.

Saddle of Lamb

YOU WILL NEED: Garlic
    Lamb   Eggs
    Butter   Brandy
    Cream sauce   Salt
    Heavy cream   Pepper

Brush the meat lightly with melted butter and place on a fireproof earthenware dish in a 375° oven, allowing 10 minutes per pound. Baste every 15 minutes. Mix in blender 1½ cups cream sauce (see page 97), ½ cup heavy cream, 1 clove garlic, the yolks of 3 eggs and ½ cup brandy. Salt and pepper the roast 10 minutes before serving. Add the sauce only long enough to heat. Stir it carefully into the pan gravy, dissolving glaze, so that it does not boil. Be prepared for compliments.

Crown of Lamb

Says Alice Toklas: "I make curl papers to place on each rib as a Sunday meeting embellishment. Cut in fringes in double paper and hold to the side of the ribs with a speck of flour diluted with a drop of water. A friend held together those she made with library paste, adding an unexpected wintergreen flavoring."

YOU WILL NEED:
> Lamb chops
> Madeira or dry white port
> Veal or chicken bouillon
> Salt and pepper
> Green peas

Have 2 ends of the undivided lamb chops, with nothing but the skin removed, tied together. This will form the crown when they are placed with the ribs standing in the air. Cover the ends of the bones with foil so they will not burn. Place the roast in a fireproof earthenware serving dish in a 400° oven allowing 40 minutes for roasting. Baste 3 times with ¾ cup Madeira or dry white port and ¾ cup veal or chicken bouillon. Add salt and pepper 10 minutes before serving. Remove foil from ribs, skim pan gravy. Fill the center of the crown with green peas.

Stuffed Breast of Mutton

It is difficult to find in the United States the infant lamb that is sold in France and was much better known here in the late

Victorian and Edwardian eras. Nowadays what we buy as lamb would be called young mutton in France. So you may, when you wish to try this recipe, ask your butcher for breast of lamb.

YOU WILL NEED:

Breast of mutton	Salt
Oysters	Ground peppers
Rosemary	Eggs
Thyme	Madeira
Parsley	Butter

This is my adaptation of an Elizabethan recipe.

Have your butcher remove the bones from a breast of mutton and make a pouch between the skin and the meat large enough to hold the dressing. Drain the water from 3 pints of oysters. Mix 1 teaspoon powdered rosemary, 1 teaspoon powdered thyme, 1 teaspoon chopped parsley, 1 teaspoon salt, 1 teaspoon ground peppers, the crushed yolks of 3 hard-boiled eggs and 4 table-spoons good Madeira. Add the oysters without crushing them. Sew up the pouch securely. Paint the meat with melted butter. Bake in 375° oven, allowing 20 minutes per pound weighed before stuffing. Baste frequently. Salt and pepper 10 minutes before serving. Skim the juices in the pan and add 1 cup good Madeira.

Leg of Mutton Sultana

Without knowing the size of the roast, it is impossible to be exact about time, but for a six-pound leg of lamb you would count on about 3 hours at 325° F.

YOU WILL NEED:

Egg	Salt
Calf's liver	Pepper
Fat from beef kidneys	Juniper berries
Parsley	Leg of mutton or lamb
Onions	Butter

Dry white wine   Parsnip
Beef bouillon   Garlic
Carrot   Flour

Place in the blender at low speed 1 egg yolk, ⅓ cup cubed calf's liver measured after skin, tubes and nerves have been removed, ¾ cup cubed fat from beef kidneys, 3 stalks parsley, 2 green onions cut into inch pieces, ½ teaspoon salt, ¼ teaspoon pepper, 12 juniper berries. Blend at low speed until perfectly smooth; then turn the blender to high speed so that the mixture becomes very fine.

Have your butcher skin a leg of mutton or a good-sized leg of lamb. Paint it generously with melted butter, rub the mixture from the blender all over it, wrap in three sheets of well-buttered wax paper (or use 2 sheets of regular aluminum foil or 1 sheet of freezer foil). Fold the sheets over the meat, pinching them together so that they will be as airtight as possible. Tie or twist the ends securely. Allow to stand at room temperature two hours before putting in the oven. When the meat has been in the oven ¼ hour add ½ cup hot water to the pan.

While the meat is roasting prepare this sauce. Pour into a saucepan 3 cups good dry white wine, 3 cups beef bouillon; add 1 carrot, 1 parsnip and 1 clove garlic. Simmer uncovered 1 hour until reduced by half. Blend 1 tablespoon butter with 1 tablespoon flour and add to sauce. Cook 5 minutes and strain. Serve in sauce boat. Send mutton to table in its papers. When opening them be careful not to lose any of the juice.

POULTRY AND GAME

Capon or Chicken en Cocotte

YOU WILL NEED:
Capon or chicken	Mushrooms
Butter	Lemon
Onions	Heavy cream
Salt and pepper	Cayenne
	Curry

Brown a capon or nice chicken in 3 tablespoons butter in Dutch oven over medium flame. Add ½ pound finely chopped onions. Lower flame, cover the pot and cook slowly for ½ hour or until tender, stirring occasionally so that the chicken does not stick to the pot; the onions will help to prevent this. Baste with the juice of the chicken which will have exuded. Salt and pepper. Place the chicken on serving dish surrounded by 1 pound whole mushrooms that have been cooked for 10 minutes in a covered saucepan with 4 tablespoons butter, a squeeze of lemon juice and ½ teaspoon salt. To the juice in the pan add ¾ cup heavy cream, 2 tablespoons butter, a pinch of cayenne and a pinch of curry. Pour over chicken and serve.

Chicken Marengo

Alice Toklas admits, "This is not quite the classic recipe but well known and greatly appreciated in Paris, which creates fashions in food as well as in modes."

YOU WILL NEED:
Chicken	Onion
Olive oil	Shallots
Flour	A bouquet
	Mushrooms

Dry white wine	Pepper
Madeira	Butter
Tomato juice	Parsley
Salt	Fried croutons

Disjoint a chicken and place it in a Dutch oven in which 4 or 5 tablespoons of olive oil is boiling. Brown the pieces of chicken evenly. Add 1 tablespoon flour, 1 chopped onion, 3 chopped shallots, a bouquet and ½ pound whole mushrooms. Pour into the pot 1 cup cold dry white wine, ½ cup Madeira, ½ cup hot water and 3 tablespoons concentrated tomato juice. Reduce heat, cover pot and cook slowly but continuously for 1 hour. Remove the bouquet, add 1 teaspoon salt, ½ teaspoon pepper, and cook 15 minutes further. Then place chicken on serving dish. Add 2 tablespoons butter to juice in pot. Tip pot in all directions and pour sauce over chicken. Sprinkle with chopped parsley. Surround the chicken with fried croutons (see page 47).

Knickerbocker Suprême of Chicken

Chicken breasts are available at shops that sell poultry parts and also come quick frozen in neat packages. The frozen chicken breasts need not be completely thawed but only enough to enable you to remove the bone and do a little shaping. Meat is easier to trim when cold or partially frozen.

YOU WILL NEED:

Chickens	Butter
Salt and pepper	Boiled ham
Heavy cream	Asparagus tips
Flour	Sauce suprême

Cut the breast meat of 3 chickens in the shape of cutlets. Sprinkle with salt and pepper and brush liberally with heavy cream and roll in flour. Fry in skillet over medium heat in 6 tablespoons melted butter, until lightly browned on both sides. Remove to a buttered preheated fireproof earthenware dish. Add juice from skillet, 1 teaspoon salt, ½ teaspoon pepper. Cover with buttered wax paper. Bake in 400° oven for 12 minutes. Place chicken on serving dish. Cover each cutlet with a thin slice of boiled ham, fat and skin removed, cut to shape. Place 6 hot asparagus tips on each cutlet. Serve with sauce suprême (see page 107) in sauce boat.

Fried Chicken in the English Manner

Note this recipe carefully. A worth-while "secret" is hidden therein—a tablespoonful of olive oil, added to the beaten egg into which the chicken pieces are dipped, keeps the meat from drying.

Alice Toklas says, "I don't remember who taught me that trick but it is worth remembering."

YOU WILL NEED:
	Lemon juice
Chicken	Parsley
Olive oil	Egg
Salt	Dry bread crumbs
Pepper	Clarified butter

Disjoint a chicken and put it for ½ hour in a marinade of ¼ cup olive oil, ¾ teaspoon salt, ¼ teaspoon pepper, 1 tablespoon lemon juice and 1 tablespoon chopped parsley. Turn the pieces several times. After ½ hour remove the chicken from marinade and wipe dry. Slightly beat 1 egg, add ½ teaspoon salt and 1 tablespoon olive oil. Dip the pieces of chicken one at a time in this and then completely cover with dry bread crumbs. Fry in 4 tablespoons clarified butter (see page 22). Serve with a garnish of fried parsley.

Fried Chicken in the Austrian Manner

YOU WILL NEED:
Chicken	Butter
Salt	Dry white wine
Paprika	Tomato purée

Cooked rice   Mushrooms
Boiled ham   Cucumbers

This recipe is for a young frying chicken, which will serve 2 persons. Season the chicken with 1 teaspoon salt and 1 teaspoon paprika. Fry in skillet in 3 tablespoons butter, turning on all sides. They will be cooked in 20 minutes. Remove to serving dish. Pour ½ cup hot dry white wine and 2 tablespoons tomato purée into skillet. Stir any glaze there may be and pour over the chickens. Place 1 cup cooked rice, in which ½ cup chopped boiled ham has been heated, at either end of dish. Garnish with fried mushrooms and simmered cucumbers.

Slice 2 large unpeeled cucumbers and place in shallow dish, cover with ⅓ teaspoon salt and let stand for 1 hour. Drain and wipe dry. Sauté in 4 tablespoons melted butter. Do not brown but simmer ¼ hour over low heat and serve hot.

Chicken in the Polish Manner

YOU WILL NEED:

Chicken   Butter
Bread   Salt
Bouillon   Paprika
Mushrooms   Egg
Boiled ham   Lemon juice
Parsley   Bread crumbs

Take a fine chicken and stuff it as follows: Soak 1 cup bread in hot bouillon for 15 minutes. Press until all the moisture has been extracted. Add 1 cup finely chopped mushrooms, 1 cup finely chopped boiled ham (fat removed) and 1 tablespoon finely chopped parsley. Place these with 4 tablespoons butter in a skillet over medium heat. Stir for 10 minutes, adding ½ teaspoon salt and 1 teaspoon paprika. Remove from heat, add 1 egg. Mix well and put in the cavity of the bird. Skewer tightly. Put the chicken in a roasting pan in a 400° oven for 45 minutes, turning and basting frequently. Ten minutes before removing from oven sprinkle with 1 teaspoon salt and 1 teaspoon paprika.

When cooked add a squeeze of lemon juice and pour over chicken 4 tablespoons browned butter mixed with 4 tablespoons freshly grated bread crumbs.

Chicken Stuffed with Sea Food

This recipe calls for a fine chicken with all accessories, including neck, liver, gizzard, tips of wings and feet.

But Miss Toklas was reminded, "Feet rarely appear on the modern American bird."

She answered, "If you have not the habit of seeing and using the feet, do not be discouraged but do as all continentals do, remember that gelatin is made from feet."

So simply ignore her directions for dealing with the feet and add to the giblet bouillon an envelope of Knox gelatin.

YOU WILL NEED:	Bouquet
Chicken	Butter
Carrot	Dry white wine
Onion	Shrimps
Cloves	Olive oil
Leek	Rice
Parsley	Fat salt pork
Thyme	Flour
Bay leaf	Giblet bouillon
Mace	Tomato paste
Peppercorns	Salt
Mussels	Pepper

For 6 people choose a fine 4-pound chicken which must include its neck, liver, gizzard, tips of wings and feet. Clean the feet by placing them directly over hot flame until the skin is burned. With the dull edge of a knife scrape off the skin. Holding a toe in the left hand with a cloth in the right hand pull off the nails. The skin and the nails are, of course, discarded. Wash the feet and the giblets thoroughly in cold water. Rinse well before placing them in a saucepan of cold water over high flame.

With a perforated spoon skim as soon as a scum rises. Then add to the saucepan 1 carrot, 1 onion stuck with 2 cloves, 1 leek, 2 stalks parsley, a twig of thyme, ½ bay leaf, 1 blade of mace and 6 peppercorns. Cover and boil slowly but steadily for 2 hours. Put 1 quart mussels in covered saucepan with a bouquet, 2 tablespoons butter and ¼ cup dry white wine. Bring to a boil. Remove from heat in 3 minutes. Drain but keep the liquid. Remove mussels from shells. Discard shells and keep mussels for later use.

Boil ½ pound shrimps until they are pink. Drain, shell and de-vein them. Keep the water in which shrimps have boiled.

Chop 1 onion and brown it in 2 tablespoons olive oil, add ½ cup rice. Stir over low flame for 5 minutes and add the liquid (strained) in which the mussels were cooked and the shrimp water. Cover and reduce heat to low. Cook for 15 minutes. Brown the liver in 1 tablespoon butter and 10 small squares of fat salt pork. Mix these with 1 cup boiled rice, mussels and shrimps. Fill the cavity of the chicken with them and skewer carefully. In a saucepan prepare a dark roux (see page 96) of 2 tablespoons butter, 2 tablespoons flour and 2 cups of the giblet bouillon. Add 1 tablespoon tomato paste.

Place 4 tablespoons butter in roasting pan. Roast the chicken in it in a 400° oven for 45 minutes. Commence to baste after 20 minutes and then baste every 10 minutes. Turn the chicken on its sides to brown. After 40 minutes add 1 teaspoon salt and ½ teaspoon pepper. Skim the juice in the pan and stir in the roux sauce. When it is hot serve around the chicken. Do not forget to remove skewers.

This is a mirific way to prepare a chicken.

Pigeons à la Toscana

If there are no pigeons in your supermarket and the dovecotes are deserted, you may with great effect use Rock Cornish game hens. They may be quick frozen but they should not be stuffed.

YOU WILL NEED: *Garlic*
    Pigeons   *Curry powder*
    Olive oil   *Cayenne*
    Salt   *Parmesan cheese*
    Pepper   *Bread crumbs*

This is a gastronomic feast which is out of all proportion to the effort of preparing it.

Pigeons in Florence 45 years ago were not the giant luscious birds of the United States of today, so to devise this way to cook them was highly intelligent. Everything combines to make them a succulent dish which they had not the possibility of becoming when taken from their dovecote.

Brown them in a Dutch oven over medium heat, allowing 1½ tablespoons olive oil for each pigeon. Cover and cook slowly for 1 hour. Add ½ teaspoon salt and ¼ teaspoon pepper and a crushed garlic per pigeon. Remove from pot and place in casserole. Sprinkle with ¼ teaspoon curry powder, a pinch of cayenne and ¼ cup grated Parmesan cheese. Dot with olive oil and dried bread crumbs. Place in 400° oven for 12 minutes.

Deep gratitude to old Maddalena who prepared this for us in those happy days.

Squabs Crapaudine

YOU WILL NEED:
    Squabs   *Green onion*
    Olive oil   *Mushrooms*
    Salt   *White onion*
    Pepper   *Dry white wine*
    Parsley   *Bouillon*

Cut the squabs the length of the breasts, pound them flat without breaking the bones, and they will look like their name (toad). Marinate them for at least 12 hours in olive oil, allowing ⅓ cup per squab, ½ teaspoon salt, ¼ teaspoon pepper, several stalks of parsley and 1 chopped green onion. Turn them several times.

When time to cook remove from marinade, pour the marinade
into a Dutch oven over medium heat. When the oil commences
to bubble place the squabs in the pot and cover. Reduce the heat
and cook undisturbed for 20 minutes, shaking the pot several
times. Then add, for each squab, ¼ pound chopped mushrooms
and continue to cook slowly. Pound 1 diced onion and 2 tablespoons dry white wine through a sieve with ¼ cup bouillon.
Baste every 10 minutes with this. It will take 1 hour in all to
cook the squabs. Remove them to serving dish. Strain the juice
and skim it before pouring over squabs.

Perfumed Goose

YOU WILL NEED: *Cloves*
   Light brown sugar   *Sage*
   Salt   *Goose*
   Cinnamon   *Apples*
   Allspice   *Lemon*
   White pepper   *Brandy*

   Mix ⅔ cup light brown sugar, 2 teaspoons salt, ½ teaspoon
powdered cinnamon, ½ teaspoon allspice, ½ teaspoon ground
white pepper, ½ teaspoon powdered cloves and ½ teaspoon
powdered sage. Beat these in 4 cups water 10 minutes. Pour
into roasting pan and place the goose in it in a 350° oven. Allow 20 minutes per pound. After 20 minutes, baste every 15
minutes, turning the goose several times. If the goose is fat it
will be necessary to skim the juice before serving.

   It is traditional to serve apples with goose. Fry stewed quartered apples sweetened with brown sugar. Add the juice of 1
lemon and 1 tablespoon brandy.

Ducks Mademoiselle
(KINDNESS OF MR. A. L. RODDES)

YOU WILL NEED:
> Ducks
> Salt and pepper
> Tokay, Concord or Muscat grapes
> Burgundy wine
> Garlic
> Butter

We like to prepare our ducks the evening before they are to be roasted.

First, sprinkle the insides freely with salt and pepper, then stuff with either Tokay, Concord or Muscat grapes, then sew up the ends.

Next, take a hypodermic needle (can purchase in any drugstore) and inject into the breasts and legs 20 or 30 injections of Burgundy wine (this softens and sweetens the meat). Rub garlic in freely from the garlic press, then paint the whole bird freely with melted butter. Place the ducks in a roasting pan and leave in refrigerator until ready to roast. Quickly roast at 450° to 500° about 30 minutes. Or if you like them well done, about 1½ to 2 hours at 325°. The meat will remain soft and tender regardless of the length of time in the oven.

Wild Duck de Hutte

The salmi of which this dish is a variant dates back to medieval times. There are those who say that a salmi of wild duck was much favored by Charlemagne.

YOU WILL NEED:
Duck	Garlic
Parsley	Salt
Shallots	Madeira
	Orange juice

Remove everything from the duck and put aside to use later. Discard gall bladder and entrails. Put the duck in a 450° oven for 20 minutes if you want it rare, as you should to enjoy it at its best.

Add to what you removed from the interior of the duck 3 stalks chopped parsley, 2 chopped shallots, 1 crushed garlic (I use an excellent little French parsley chopper for all these). Add ½ teaspoon salt, ½ cup good Madeira and ¼ cup orange juice. Stir over low heat until hot. Place duck on serving dish, prick in 4 or 5 different places and place on the top of the duck the finely chopped mixture, also finely chopped giblets which have simmered ¼ hour in ¼ cup wine. One may call this a simplified, abbreviated salmi.

Partridge with Apples in the Normandy Manner

YOU WILL NEED:

Partridge	Apples
Salt pork	Salt
Butter	Calvados or applejack brandy

Wrap the bird in a large thin slice of fat salt pork, skin removed. Brown lightly in 4 tablespoons butter in a fireproof earthenware dish. Remove bird from dish and set aside. Place in the dish 4 peeled, cored and quartered apples. Cook over low flame so that they do not scorch. In 15 minutes place the partridge on this tender mattress, surround with 4 more peeled, cored and sliced apples. Brush the partridge and apples with 4 tablespoons melted butter and bake in 350° oven for ½ hour. Before serving sprinkle with 1 teaspoon salt and pour into the pan ½ cup Calvados. If Calvados is not available, applejack may be substituted.

Venison Chops with Juniper Berries

YOU WILL NEED:

Cutlets	Pepper
Butter	Juniper berries
Gin	Croutons
Salt	Currant jelly

For 4 people place 4 cutlets in 4 tablespoons butter in hot skillet. Watch them carefully; they should be cooked in 12 minutes, rosy in the center. When cooked remove from skillet. Keep hot. Pour into skillet ½ cup good gin and scrape all the glaze from the bottom and the sides. Add 1 teaspoon salt, ⅓ teaspoon pepper and 4 crushed juniper berries. Place cutlets on croutons (see page 47) and pour juice over them. Serve currant jelly at the same time.

Rabbit Valhirmeil

Unless you have a hunting husband or live in rabbit country you may find it more convenient to buy a package of quick-frozen and already cut-up rabbit to use in this excellent recipe. Since this is a rich dish, 1 medium-sized rabbit or a package of quick-frozen rabbit should be sufficient for 6 servings.

YOU WILL NEED:

Rabbit	Onion
Thyme	Cloves
Bay leaf	Lemon
Parsley	Brandy
Salt	Olive oil
Pepper	Tomatoes
Carrots	Black olives

Wipe a rabbit with a moist cloth and cut in 8 pieces. Place in a deep dish with a sprig of thyme, a bay leaf, 3 stalks of parsley, ½ teaspoon salt, ¼ teaspoon pepper, 2 sliced carrots, 1 onion stuck with 2 cloves and 1 sliced lemon. Pour over these 1 cup brandy. Marinate for 24 hours, turning the rabbit several times.

The next day brush a saucepan (I have a weakness for the Dutch oven) generously with olive oil. Add 2 pounds tomatoes, skins and seeds removed, the pieces of rabbit and the marinade, minus the slices of lemon. Cook slowly over low heat, basting from time to time with another cup of brandy. After 2 hours remove pieces of rabbit to serving dish. Strain the sauce, place it over heat in small saucepan with 1 pound pitted black olives. As soon as it boils pour over pieces of rabbit, on which sprinkle the grated rind of 1 lemon and 1 tablespoon chopped parsley.

Nameless Rabbit

This is one case where we wouldn't presume to suggest using quick-frozen cut-up rabbit. This rabbit should come to the table dramatically—all in one piece.

YOU WILL NEED:

Rabbit	Parsley
Lemon	Green onion
Salt	Fat salt pork
Pepper	Eggs
Dry mustard	Bread

Wipe a young rabbit with a moist cloth and then with a dry one. Rub with ½ lemon and rub in 1 teaspoon salt, ½ teaspoon pepper and 1 teaspoon dry mustard. Chop the liver of the rabbit, 3 stalks parsley, 1 green onion, dice ½ cup fat salt pork, rind removed, crush the yolks of 2 hard-boiled eggs. Mix all these ingredients well and stuff the body of the rabbit with them. Sew the skin over the stuffing carefully so that none of it will escape while roasting. Cut pieces of bread in slices ¾ inches thick to completely cover the back and sides of the rabbit. Cover the bread with thin slices of fat salt pork. Be sure the rabbit is entirely covered and tie securely. Cover the rabbit with 2 well-buttered sheets of wax paper. Roast in fireproof earthenware dish in 375° oven for 45 minutes. Discard paper and strings. Add 1 tablespoon lemon juice to pan gravy and serve. Succulent. Remove bread and pork and cut into pieces suitable for serving.

COOKING WITH CHAMPAGNE

"Why not cook with champagne," said a friend, "since in California you drank it in the morning and the maids picked up diamonds when cleaning after parties?"

"Yes," I answered feebly, for we did drink champagne in the morning, at least a generation before the champagne cocktail had been created, and once a diamond had been found on the floor after a party.

When I came to Paris, the first dish I learned to cook with champagne was:

Braised Capon

If you do not want to go to the trouble of boiling artichokes and removing the hearts, you may substitute a package of frozen artichoke hearts. And when the fresh vegetable is not in season, canned or frozen asparagus tips may be used.

YOU WILL NEED:

Chicken or capon	Dry champagne
Salt	Artichokes
Lemon	Asparagus tips
Butter	New potatoes

Rub a capon (if you can find one and can afford it; if not, a fine big chicken) on all sides with half a lemon. This will keep the flesh white. Then rub in ½ teaspoon salt. Melt ¼ cup butter in a saucepan with a tight-fitting cover. When the butter is melted, place the capon in the saucepan and heat it on all sides, but without browning. Reduce heat, cover. After 15 minutes, raise heat and add 1½ cups dry champagne. Cover, lower heat and cook gently for 45 minutes. During this time, boil 4 large artichokes for about 30 minutes, depending upon their size. When a leaf can be easily removed, take from heat, drain and remove leaves, leaving the hearts. (The leaves can be scraped later and used in an omelette.) Also, boil in salted water ¾ pound green asparagus tips. Do not overboil, but when sufficiently tender, drain. Boil 1 pound very small new potatoes, add to the casserole. After the juice boils up again, place the fowl in a preheated serving dish surrounded by the artichoke hearts, asparagus and new potatoes.

Hare Simmered in Champagne

A young hare is not always available in all parts of the United States—and that's an understatement. But it is not too difficult to get quick-frozen rabbit cut into serving pieces as for fricassee and neatly arranged in a package. While the effect is not quite so dramatic as a whole hare on a platter, the taste is fine and the cooking time will be only 1 or 1½ instead of 2 hours.

YOU WILL NEED:

Hare	Bay leaf
Salt	Thyme
Pepper	Parsley
Salt pork	Dry champagne
Butter	Cognac
Onions	Truffles
Shallots	Heavy cream
Garlic	Toasted bread or puff pastry

Rub a young hare with 1 tablespoon salt and ½ teaspoon pepper. Cover with thin slices of fat salt pork, tie lightly. Then tie the hare firmly into a round—the forelegs first, then the hind legs and finally the head to the hind quarters. Put ⅓ cup butter in a large round Dutch oven with 2 chopped onions, 5 chopped shallots and 2 cloves crushed garlic with a bouquet of ½ bay leaf, a sprig of thyme and some parsley. As soon as the butter bubbles, place the hare in the Dutch oven, cover tightly, reduce heat and cook very slowly for 2 hours, turning occasionally.

Reduce by half over low flame 1 quart dry champagne. When reduced, set it on fire together with ½ cup very good cognac and pour over hare, allowing it to simmer 1 hour longer. Meanwhile, simmer 5 fine truffles in 1 cup champagne for 1 hour. Cut in slices and add to juice in Dutch oven. Place hare on preheated serving dish, remove strings. To contents of the pot, from which all grease has been skimmed, add 6 tablespoons heavy cream. Heat thoroughly, but do not allow to boil. Strain over hare and serve at once. The hare may be surrounded by lightly toasted pieces of bread, with crusts removed, or small crescents of puff pastry.

Kidneys in Champagne

Kidneys are strange things. In order to be tender they must be cooked a very short or a long time. The trick is to cook them briefly, but if by mischance you should overcook, you can eventually bring them back to eatability but never to their original juiciness by simmering them slowly for about 2 hours. So it pays to be wary and quick with your fork.

YOU WILL NEED:
>Pigs' kidneys or veal kidneys
>>or chicken livers
>Onions
>Shallots
>Garlic
>Parsley
>Butter
>Flour
>Dry champagne

Allow one pig's kidney per person. For 4 kidneys chop ⅓ cup onion and 3 shallots and crush 1 clove garlic. Put aside 2 tablespoons very finely chopped parsley. Cut the kidneys in half lengthwise, remove all skin, fat and nerves.

Over high heat melt ½ cup butter. When it bubbles, add the chopped onions, shallots and garlic; then the kidneys. Turn with wooden or stainless steel or silver fork. When the kidneys are no longer red (after about 2 minutes) add 2 tablespoons flour. Turning over very high heat, cook 2 minutes and then add 1½ cups dry champagne. Continue cooking for 2 or 3 minutes. Pour into preheated serving dish and sprinkle chopped parsley over the top. The kidneys should not cook more than 10 minutes. With deftness, 8 minutes should suffice.

If pigs' kidneys are not tempting, try veal kidneys. If all kidneys are anathema, chicken livers can be substituted successfully.

Shellfish in Champagne Sauce

This recipe does not require a great deal of time but there is no denying it is a Production. Resplendent enough to repay you mightily!

| YOU WILL NEED: | Crabs |
| Lobsters | Shrimp |

For the court bouillon:

Carrots	Thyme
Onions	Parsley
Bay leaf	Whole black pepper

For the sauce:

Butter	Flour
Onion	Salt
Shallots	Heavy cream
Eggs	Champagne

Use about equal quantities of lobster, crab and shrimp—say a 2-pound lobster, a 2-pound crab and 1½ pounds shrimps. Make a court bouillon using 2 carrots, 2 onions, 1 bay leaf, sprig of thyme, several stalks of parsley, several whole black peppers and enough water to float the lobster. Cook a few minutes. Add lobster and simmer 25 minutes or until done. Cook the crab in the same bouillon in the same way.

Boil shrimps in water just long enough to have them turn pink. Cut the lobster in half lengthwise, remove meat, crack the claws and remove meat. Put the meat aside. From the shell remove and discard sack. Scrape everything else from shell and put aside. Prepare crab in same manner. Shell shrimps and remove black vein from back. Cut the lobster and crab meat in neat slices and mix with shrimps. Strain through a sieve, or put into your blender, scrapings from the lobster and crab shells. Melt ⅓ cup butter in a saucepan over medium heat, add 1 finely chopped onion and 2 finely chopped shallots. Cook for 10 minutes but do not allow to brown. Add lobster, crab meat and shrimps and ½ teaspoon salt. To strained or blended scrapings of the shells, stir in, one at a time, the yolks of 3 eggs and 1 tablespoon flour. Stir until perfectly smooth. Add 6 tablespoons heavy cream. Pour into saucepan 2 cups champagne, bring to boil; reduce heat and add scrapings, egg-and-cream mixture, and the crab, lobster slices and shrimps. Do not allow to boil but turn constantly in the same direction until sauce is hot and has thickened. Serve at once.

Sweetbread Salad

Nutmeg melons suggested in this recipe do not seem to be available in our markets. At least I have never been able to find them in New York or Connecticut. Miss Toklas suggests using small cantaloupes instead, or you might try Spanish melon or casaba. The melon should be firm, not at all mushy and not too sweet. This is a supper salad adequate to serve 3 or 4 people.

YOU WILL NEED: *Peppercorns*
    Sweetbreads   *Parsley*
    Salt   *Bay leaf*

Thyme	*Nutmeg melons or small*
Onion	*cantaloupes*
Carrot	*Mushrooms*
Lemon juice	*Lemon*
Cucumber	*Champagne*
Tomatoes	*Lettuce*

A very exotic dish that is always greeted with surprise. Soak a pair of sweetbreads in cold water for 1 hour. Rinse in fresh water. Place in saucepan, cover with water, add ½ tablespoon salt, 4 peppercorns and a bouquet of parsley, ½ bay leaf and a small sprig of thyme, a small onion, 1 carrot and 1 teaspoon lemon juice. Simmer, covered, for 30 minutes. Remove sweetbreads from saucepan, drain and wipe dry. As soon as they are cool enough to handle, remove skin, fat and tendons. Slice neatly in 6 fillets.

Peel a cucumber, slice and sprinkle salt fairly liberally over the slices. Blanch 3 firm tomatoes, remove skins and slice. Cut 3 nutmeg melons or small cantaloupes in half, remove seeds and fibers, cut in slices and remove rinds.

Boil for 12 minutes ½ pound sliced mushrooms in 1 cup water to which the juice of ½ lemon has been added. Place the sweetbreads on a bed of lettuce in the center of a flat dish. Arrange around them the sliced cucumbers, which have been carefully wiped dry and free of salt, the tomatoes, mushrooms and sliced melons. Pour over 1½ cups chilled champagne.

Choucroute and Fluetters

A pig's trotter (in case your butcher should be confused) is of course nothing but a pig's foot. You may have to tell your butcher a day or two ahead of time that you want one especially if you live in a neighborhood where feet, tails, etc., are not generally used. As for smoked pork chops, you can find them at German delicatessens in some of our larger cities or use smoked shoulder cut into slices or left in a hunk.

This is the kind of recipe where almost every ingredient except the sauerkraut can be altered to suit the needs and provisions of the moment.

Choucroute

YOU WILL NEED:
Sauerkraut
Fat salt pork
Pig's trotter
Pork rind, lean pork
   and breast of pork
Juniper berries
Whole black peppers
Cloves
Bay leaf

Thyme
Onions
Garlic
Beef bouillon
Champagne
Fresh pork chops
Smoked pork chops
Frankfurt sausages
Strasburg sausages
Sliced ham

This is a distinguished version of a common dish. Line the bottom of an enameled pot that has a tight-fitting cover with slices of fat salt pork. On this place a fresh pig's trotter, ½ pound of pork rind with a half inch of lean pork. Add 1 pound uncooked sauerkraut, 1 pound breast of pork cut into 6 pieces. In a cheesecloth bag place ¼ cup juniper berries, 10 whole black peppers, 2 whole cloves, 1 bay leaf, and a sprig of thyme. Then add 2 chopped onions and 2 crushed cloves of garlic, 2 cups of good beef bouillon and 2 cups of champagne. Cover, bring to a boil and simmer for 5 hours. Be careful nothing sticks to the pot. Remove from heat and when quite cold remove all fat. It is a good idea to let it stand overnight. After the fat, trotter, rind, and the bag of spices have been removed, bring to a boil again and add 4 fresh pork chops and 4 smoked pork chops. Simmer for 1 hour; add 4 slices of ham from which the fat has been removed, 4 Frankfurt sausages and 4 Strasburg sausages and cook 10 minutes. Serve very hot with:

Fluetters

YOU WILL NEED:

Potatoes	Parsley
Flour	Garlic
Salt	Eggs
Pepper	Butter

Boil 2 pounds peeled potatoes cut in quarters in enough salted water to cover. Mash thoroughly. Add 2 tablespoons flour, ½ teaspoon salt, ¼ teaspoon pepper, 2 tablespoons very finely chopped parsley, 1 clove crushed garlic and 2 whole eggs. Beat until smooth. Form into 10 or 12 balls and place on well-buttered fireproof earthenware dish. Paint with ⅓ cup melted butter and brown in oven for 20 minutes. This is an Alsatian way to prepare potatoes and consequently a fitting accompaniment to a dish of choucroute.

Champagne Punch

The popular taste over the past years inclines always toward lighter and drier—less sweet—drinks. It is possible that you would prefer to use only one cup rather than 2 cups of sugar. You can always add more at the last moment.

YOU WILL NEED:

Sugar	Lemons
Green Chinese tea	Oranges
Pineapple	Curaçao or cointreau
Tokay wine	Dry champagne
	Strawberries

This is an excellent punch served in California for festive occasions.

Boil 2 cups sugar with ¾ cup water for 5 minutes. Pour 1½ cups boiling water over 2 heaping teaspoons of green Chinese tea. Let stand 3 minutes, strain and put aside to cool. Slice a medium-sized pineapple. Cut each slice into 8 pieces, remove rough center and eyes and put them into a saucepan with the scrapings from the shell. Cover with water, add 1 cup sugar and simmer for 20 minutes. Strain through a fine sieve. Squeeze the juice from 5 lemons and 6 oranges.

Combine pineapple slices with syrup and fruit juices. Add 1 bottle Tokay and 1 cup white curaçao or cointreau. Let stand for 4 hours. Then add 2 quarts dry champagne and 1 pint well-chosen strawberries. Pour over a block of ice into punch bowl. Makes 5 quarts, about forty 4-ounce servings.

These are royal dishes. It was said long ago that good Californians, when they die, do not go to Heaven, but go to Paris. Are not these recipes part of the reward?

COOKING WITH COGNAC

It has been my habit for several years to keep a carafe of good cognac on a kitchen shelf. Like salt, it brings out and amalgamates the various flavors of any dish.

Here are recipes requiring more than 1 or 2 tablespoons of cognac, lighted or not:

Onion Soup

Consider that this is said in a whisper: You can use Miss Toklas' ideas even though you resort to canned or packaged dehydrated onion soup. Use her croutons covered each with a slice of Swiss cheese. Add ½ cup cognac to 6 cups of soup which has been prepared in the usual way according to package directions.

YOU WILL NEED:
    Onions
    Butter
    Sugar
    French bread

Swiss cheese
Beef bouillon
Cognac
Salt and pepper
Parmesan cheese

Put 4 sliced onions in a saucepan in which 4 tablespoons butter are bubbling. Sprinkle 1 teaspoon sugar over the onions. In about 10 minutes, when they are golden, not browned, remove from heat. Cut 1 pound French bread in ⅓-inch slices and toast them. They are now croutons. Butter them generously and cover each with a slice of Swiss cheese.

Place the onions in a large fireproof earthenware dish and pour over them 6 cups hot beef bouillon, ½ cup cognac, salt

75

and pepper and the prepared bread. Place in a preheated moderately hot oven for 20 minutes. Serve piping hot and pass grated Parmesan cheese. This is an onion soup with a distinct difference and you will find it an excellent one with which to start a meal.

Omelette with Chicken-Liver Paste

A quick version of this omelette may be prepared by using 4-ounce tins of Sell's liver pâté. Melt 1 tablespoon butter, add the liver pâté along with ½ cup cognac and stir till just heated through over a low flame. Keep warm and proceed with the making of the omelette.

YOU WILL NEED: *Salt*
   Chicken livers   *Butter*
   Cognac   *Eggs*

This is the recipe for the famous omelette of La Mère Poularde of Mont-Saint-Michel. To commence with the chicken-liver paste, which is my contribution, cook ¾ pound chicken livers in ½ cup cognac over low flame. Add ¼ teaspoon salt and 1 tablespoon butter. Cover but stir once or twice to prevent scorching. They will be sufficiently cooked in about 12 minutes. Test with the point of a sharp knife to see that it is juice, not blood, that exudes. Then pound through a sieve and keep hot in a covered pan while the omelette is being prepared.

Beat 6 eggs with a pinch of salt for 5 minutes with a rotary beater or 2 minutes in a blender until they are quite thick. During this time heat a piece of butter about the size of an egg in a heavy saucepan. The butter should be golden when you pour in the eggs. In ¼ minute (is a stop watch among your kitchen utensils?) stir the omelette with a long-handled fork. The pan should be very hot. In ¾ of a minute (the stop watch to the rescue again) lift a corner of the omelette and add another piece of butter the size of an egg. The omelette will be cooked in 1 minute (here the kitchen clock will suffice). At once, spoon the liver paste on the omelette. Fold the omelette over and serve immediately on a warm but not hot plate.

Sweet Potatoes and Oranges au Cognac

To save time, canned sweet potatoes may be used. And since they are already cooked you may turn the oven up a little higher, to about 375° F., and cook 5 or 10 minutes less or until they are well heated and lightly browned. Makes 6 servings.

YOU WILL NEED: *Brown sugar*
 Sweet potatoes *Oranges*
 Butter   *Cognac*

Boil 6 sweet potatoes in their jackets until they are not quite tender. Peel, slice, put a layer in a buttered ovenproof dish, dot with butter, sprinkle with brown sugar, cover with a layer of thinly sliced unpeeled oranges from which seeds and the white center have been removed. Continue in this manner until the 6 potatoes and 2 large oranges, ½ cup brown sugar and ⅓ cup butter have been used. Pour over the contents of the dish ½ cup cognac. Sprinkle over the top brown sugar and dot with butter. Bake about ½ hour or until well browned in medium oven (350°). Serve hot with pork, roasted or grilled.

Boeuf à la Mode

Miss Toklas suggests that in this case you must do the larding yourself because the strips of fat salt pork must first soak 4 or 5 hours in cognac. Even if larding were not so old-fashioned, butchers are few and far between who remember or care any longer to practice the art of wielding the larding needle. Even the needles are hard to find. Alice Toklas sent me two from Paris, where she had found them in Deladier's, near Les Halles.

They are available at the Bazaar Française, 666 Avenue of the Americas, New York City.

If you have a freezer you might prepare two 5-pound pieces of beef at the same time. Use one and put the other away in the freezer, but don't plan to keep it there more than a month or two. The spicing has a tendency to become too intense.

YOU WILL NEED:
Top round of beef	*Mace*
Dry white wine	*Thyme*
Cognac	*Ginger*
Fat salt pork	*Butter*
Parsley	*Beef bouillon*
Basil	*Carrots*
Salt	*Onions*
Pepper	*Bay leaf*
Cloves	*Calf's foot or Knox gelatin*
	Eggs

Marinate 5 pounds top round of beef for 24 hours in 1 bottle good dry white wine and 1 cup good cognac, turning the meat several times. The next day remove meat from its bath and dry thoroughly. You will do the larding, for your butcher can't do it for you, because the strips of fat salt pork must soak for 4 or 5 hours in cognac. Each strip, after it has been placed in the larding needle, must have rubbed into it a mixture of some finely chopped parsley, some powdered basil, salt, pepper, a good pinch of cloves, mace and thyme all well mixed. Push the larding needle into the meat with the grain of the meat at 8 or 9 evenly separated places. Allow the lardons to extend ¾ inch beyond the meat on either end. Rub into the meat 1 tablespoon salt, 1 teaspoon pepper, ½ teaspoon ginger and ¼ teaspoon mace. Put 4 tablespoons butter in a heavy enameled pot and brown the meat gently on all sides. Pour ½ cup lighted cognac over it. Remove meat and line the pot with a piece of fat salt pork about ¾ inch thick with rind included. Place the meat on it and pour over it the marinade brought to a boil with 1 cup beef bouillon, ½ pound sliced carrots, 2 large sliced onions, a bouquet of parsley, thyme and bay leaf and a calf's foot washed in hot water and thoroughly scraped. Cover and bring to a quick boil. Reduce heat and simmer for 4½ hours. Remove meat and carrots to preheated shallow serving dish. Skim sauce and strain over meat. (If you haven't a calf's foot handy, use 2 envelopes of Knox gelatin to give the needed gelatinous texture to the sauce.)

This is a succulent dish and is equally delicious cold, in which case the juice must be clarified. To do this, heat the juice over medium flame along with 2 whites of eggs and 2 eggshells. When it comes to a boil remove from heat, let stand for 20 minutes. Then strain through a moistened piece of muslin.

The meat is sliced and the slices placed overlapping in a deep bowl. When the juice is cold and as thick as cream, pour it over the meat and place the bowl in the refrigerator. Unmold in the usual way.

Half of the beef may be eaten hot the first day and the rest cold another day. As there will then be half of the sauce to clarify, use 1 white of egg and 1 egg shell.

Short Ribs of Beef

If in your supermarket a beef knuckle and a calf's foot should be difficult to get, simply forget the knuckle and add 2 envelopes Knox gelatin. This will give to the gravy the gelatinous feel that it should have. Four pounds of ribs will make only about 4 servings. You can double or triple the recipe while you are about it. Any leftovers will freeze admirably.

YOU WILL NEED:

Short ribs of beef	Pepper
Fat salt pork	Ginger
Onions	Cinnamon
Carrots	Parsley
Beef knuckle	Bay leaf
Salt	Thyme

　　　Cognac　　　　　　　　*Beef bouillon*
　　　Madeira or sherry　　*Calf's foot*

Have the butcher separate 4 pounds short ribs of beef. Tie them together but not too tightly. Cover the bottom of a Dutch oven with slices of fat salt pork. Place on top of pork 2 sliced onions and 1 pound sliced carrots. Place the short ribs on this with 1 pound of beef knuckle in several pieces. Add 1 teaspoon of salt, ½ teaspoon pepper, a good pinch of ginger and of cinnamon, and a bouquet of parsley, 1 bay leaf and a twig of thyme. Place over low heat, covered, for 20 minutes so that the meat will exude its juice. Then add ¾ cup cognac and ½ cup Madeira or sherry and enough beef bouillon to cover the short ribs. Then add ½ calf's foot which has been washed in hot water and scraped. Place the Dutch oven hermetically covered in a preheated 350° F. oven for 3½ hours. Turn the meat twice. The meat will be quite tender, what the French call "fondant" (melting).

Remove from oven, place short ribs on preheated oven-proof dish, pour strained juice over them. Put in hot oven to glaze, about 10 minutes. This dish requires a green vegetable, braised lettuce, for instance.

Fried Spring Chicken Flambé

YOU WILL NEED:
　　　Broilers　　　　*Pepper*
　　　Lemon　　　　　*Pinch nutmeg*
　　　Egg　　　　　　*Bread crumbs*
　　　Olive oil　　　　*Butter*
　　　Salt　　　　　　*Cognac*

This is a 1939 way to prepare fried chicken. Wipe 2 broilers with a moist cloth, dry them and rub with half a lemon. This will keep them white. Disjoint them. Keep backs and wings to make a bouillon. Cover the pieces of chicken with 1 beaten egg to which have been added 1 tablespoon olive oil, 1 teaspoon salt,

¼ teaspoon pepper and a pinch of nutmeg. Cover each piece completely with fine dry bread crumbs.

In a heavy frying pan heat ¼ cup butter and add ¼ cup olive oil. Lightly brown the pieces of the chicken, being careful not to disturb the egg-and-crumb coating. Add 1 cup lighted cognac. Lower the flame and cover the pan. Shake the pan frequently so chicken will not scorch. In ½ hour it will be ready to serve with oyster sauce (recipe follows).

Oyster Sauce

YOU WILL NEED:

Truffles	Salt
Parsley	Pepper
Shallot	Oysters
Green onion	Cognac
Butter	Chicken bouillon

Slice 3 truffles and put aside. Chop another truffle very fine with 3 stalks parsley, 1 shallot and 1 green onion. Pound through a fine sieve. Mix with ½ cup soft but not melted butter. Add ½ teaspoon salt and ⅛ teaspoon pepper and put aside.

Allow 2 dozen oysters to come just to the boil in their juice. Drain and keep the juice. Brush a saucepan with the truffle-butter mixture. Place half of the sliced truffles on the bottom of the saucepan. Dot with ⅓ of the remaining truffle-butter mixture. Then add a layer of all the oysters, dot with truffle butter, add the rest of the sliced truffles and top with all of the remaining truffle butter. Cover and keep hot but do not allow to boil. Skim excess butter and add oyster juice, ½ cup cognac and ¼ cup chicken bouillon. Bring slowly to a boil. Remove chicken from frying pan to preheated serving dish. Add a little of the hot sauce to pan and stir to thoroughly mix. Add to sauce, beat well and pour over chicken. Serve at once.

Roast Chicken with Olives

Cooking on a spit is something of an undertaking in a Paris apartment but no trouble at all in the United States where we have our electric rotisseries. This is a delightful change from the usual barbecue.

YOU WILL NEED:
Roasting chicken	Bread crumbs
Fat salt pork or bacon	Flour
Butter	Cognac
Chicken bouillon	Bay leaf
Parsley	Thyme
Green onion	Olive oil
Lard	Green olives
Eggs	Anchovy
	Tips of asparagus

This is a still older (1691) recipe. Entirely cover the breast of a fine roasting chicken with large thin slices of fat salt pork (rind removed), or use bacon. Tie securely but not too tightly in place. Put the chicken in a roasting pan or better still on a spit. In the dripping pan put ½ cup butter and ½ cup chicken bouillon, and baste chicken as it cooks. In a saucepan place 3 stalks of parsley, 1 diced green onion, 2 tablespoons lard and 1 tablespoon flour. When the lard commences to bubble, add the contents of the dripping pan, bring to a boil and add ½ cup hot chicken bouillon, ½ cup cognac, 1 bay leaf, a twig of thyme, 1 tablespoon olive oil, 12 pitted and finely chopped green olives and 1 crushed anchovy. Cover and simmer for 15 minutes. Then add little by little another ½ cup hot chicken bouillon. When the chicken is done place on a preheated shallow serving dish. Strain the sauce and reheat. Pour a little of it into the pan (if the chicken has not been cooked on a spit), and stir to release any of the juice adhering to the pan. Add this to the sauce and skim the sauce. Pour sauce over chicken. Surround by green tips of asparagus lightly cooked and sprinkled with

2 chopped hard-cooked eggs mixed with fine bread crumbs browned in butter.

Stuffed Duck

YOU WILL NEED:

Eggs	Cayenne
Heavy cream	Nutmeg
Beef fat from kidney	Duck
Mushrooms	Beef bouillon
Onions (green)	Cognac
Salt	Purée of chestnuts
Pepper	White wine
	Butter

With the miracle-working blender, preparation of this next recipe is cut in half.

Place in the blender at lowest speed 2 eggs, ½ cup heavy cream, ¼ cup cubed beef fat from the kidney, ¼ pound cubed mushrooms, 2 diced green onions, ¼ teaspoon salt, ⅛ teaspoon pepper, a pinch of cayenne and a pinch of nutmeg. Blend first at low speed until smooth and then at high speed until very fine.

Now for the duck: Remove the wings and legs, cutting into the skin as little as possible, and put them aside. You will now bone the duck. To do this cut the skin down the back and, with the aid of a small sharp knife, loosen the skin from the meat, rolling it back gently without piercing it. Go easy the first time you skin a fowl. The cook who taught me did it as easily as he skinned a rabbit or an eel. When it has been accomplished, remove all the meat from the bones, slice the filets and cut the rest of the meat as nicely as possible; put aside. Place the skin flat on the table, place the wings and legs in their proper places and sew the skin around them. Neatly arrange the filets and meat on the skin, leaving a margin on all four sides. Then spread the stuffing on the meat. Sew the skin down the back and at both ends. You now have a boned stuffed duck ready to be braised.

In a heavy enameled pot with a tight-fitting cover, or a Dutch oven, melt 4 tablespoons butter. Over medium flame heat the duck on all sides but do *not* brown. Cover and lower flame. After 15 minutes add 1 cup beef bouillon. Heat 2 tablespoons cognac and pour it lighted over the duck. In 50 minutes the duck should be cooked. Serve without cutting the strings. Carve in slices commencing at either side. The wings and legs are placed on a slice. With the duck serve a thinned purée of chestnuts, easily made in your blender by adding a little white wine to the cooked chestnuts. (*Or use a canned purée of chestnuts from France thinned with equal parts of meat or chicken broth and white wine. P.C.*)

Duck in Delicate Aspic

This is the recipe to serve by candlelight to the strains of a minuet. Under the circumstances, it seems almost irreverent to suggest that the beef bouillon necessary for the aspic can be made from a bouillon cube or an envelope of MBT. The grated parsnip or turnip, difficult to come by in summer, is not necessary. Just use an extra carrot.

YOU WILL NEED:

Duck	Onions
Fat salt pork	Lean ham
Salt	Garlic
Pepper	Parsley
Ginger	Cloves
Mace	Cognac
Shallots	Dry white wine
Carrots	Beef bouillon
Parsnip or turnip	Orange juice

This was a favorite dish in 1797. Cover the duck with pieces of fat salt pork that has one side rubbed with salt, pepper, ginger, mace and very finely chopped shallots. Tie in place, prepared side on the duck. Cover the bottom of a Dutch oven with fat salt pork, rind removed, place the duck on it and sprinkle over the duck ½ teaspoon salt, ¼ teaspoon pepper, 2 grated carrots, 1 grated parsnip or turnip, 2 grated onions, ¼ cup chopped lean ham, 2 cloves crushed garlic, a sprig of parsley and 3 whole cloves. Pour over this 1 cup cognac, 1 cup dry white wine, 1 cup beef bouillon which has been brought to a boil. Bring to a boil, covered, over high heat and put in pre-heated 350° F. oven. (The recipe says to put the pot in hot ashes.) It will take about ¾ hour to cook the duck. Place the duck in a bowl, breast down, after having removed string. Skim the juice, add 1 tablespoon orange juice and strain the juice over the duck. Chill and unmold before serving.

Turkey Legs Revived

This is a leftover dish with grandeur or at least it was intended as such. But in these days when the parts are sometimes easier to buy than the whole, you might roast some turkey legs or even chicken legs especially for this eighteenth-century dish. Instead of the accompanying sweetbreads, you could serve rice or noodles.

YOU WILL NEED:	
Turkey legs (joints and drumsticks)	Pepper
	Parsley
	Garlic
Cognac	Green onion
Beef bouillon	Cloves
Salt	Sweetbread

This recipe is also dated 1797. Put 2 roasted turkey legs (second joints and drumsticks) in a saucepan with ¾ cup cognac, ¾ cup beef bouillon, ½ teaspoon salt, ¼ teaspoon pepper, a bouquet of 1 stalk parsley, ½ clove garlic, 1 green onion and 2 cloves. Cover and cook over medium flame until the liquid is completely absorbed.

Place the pieces of turkey on preheated serving dish and cover with stewed sweetbread, prepared while turkey is cooking.

Stewed Sweetbread

Miss Toklas suggests serving this stewed sweetbread over her turkey legs revived (see page 85). It is an interesting combination of tastes and textures. However, both dishes can stand on their own as excellent entrées to be served with rice or fine noodles and accompanied by a green vegetable.

YOU WILL NEED:

Sweetbread	Lemon juice
Salt	Parsley
Butter	Beef bouillon
Mushrooms	Cognac
Green onion	

Soak a sweetbread for 1 hour in cold water. Place in saucepan, cover with cold water, add 1 teaspoon salt, cover saucepan and bring to a boil. The sweetbread will be cooked in 20 minutes. Remove from pan and allow cold water to run over it until it is tepid, when tubes and skin should be removed and sweetbread cut in cubes.

Put 4 tablespoons butter in a saucepan. When it bubbles add cubed sweetbread, ½ pound sliced mushrooms, 1 chopped green onion and 1 tablespoon lemon juice. Stir with a wooden spoon, sprinkle 1 tablespoon parsley over this and gradually add ½ cup hot beef bouillon and ½ cup hot cognac. Simmer for 15 minutes, stirring with wooden spoon. Pour over turkey legs and serve.

Jugged Hare

This dish, which was very popular in England during the last century, probably dates back to medieval times. It is not necessary to catch your hare, clean, skin or disjoint it yourself. If your butcher is fresh out of young hares you will probably be able to find a rabbit quick frozen and cut into serving pieces in the frozen-food cabinet at your supermarket.

YOU WILL NEED:

Hare	Basil
Dry red wine	Celery
Olive oil	Bay leaves
Salt and pepper	Cloves
Butter	Shallots
Onion	Mace
Flour	Brandy
Parsley	Croutons
Thyme	Soubise sauce

Wipe the hare with a moist cloth and disjoint it. Marinate for 24 hours in following mixture: A bottle of excellent dry red wine (the better the wine the better the sauce), ½ cup olive oil, 1 teaspoon salt, ½ teaspoon pepper. Turn the pieces twice before removing from their bath the next day. Save the marinade. Dry each piece thoroughly. Brown them in 6 tablespoons butter.

In a covered saucepan cook very slowly 1 sliced onion in 1 tablespoon butter. Put 4 tablespoons butter in a Dutch oven. When it bubbles, add 1 tablespoon flour. Stir until golden brown. Add the browned pieces of hare, the cooked onions, ½ tablespoon fat, a bouquet of several stalks of parsley, thyme, basil, celery, 2 bay leaves, 3 cloves, 3 shallots and a blade of mace. Cover the pot and allow to stew in its own juice for ¼ hour over very low flame. Bring to a boil and add the marinade, which you have taken the precaution to heat. Cook gently about ¾ of an hour and then add 1½ cups of brandy. The hare, depending upon its age and size, will require about 1 hour further cooking. It should be served surrounded by toasted croutons (see page 47) covered with soubise sauce (see page 88).

Soubise Sauce

This sauce is spooned over the croutons, which are then lightly browned and crusted by being put into the oven for about 5 minutes or set under the broiler for 2 or 3 minutes.

YOU WILL NEED:

Béchamel sauce	Heavy cream
Onion juice	Salt
Very rich veal or chicken	Pepper
bouillon	Nutmeg

Make 1 cup thick béchamel sauce (see page 97). Add 2 tablespoons onion juice, 2 tablespoons very rich veal or chicken bouillon and 2 tablespoons heavy cream, salt, pepper and a pinch of nutmeg. Brown the croutons lightly in the oven or under the broiler.

Cabbage Pancakes

If you want your cabbage to keep more of its natural crisp identity, you must cook it briefly. Ten minutes may suffice, depending on your point of view. Use a small cabbage and you will have about 3 dozen pancakes, enough for six people. This is a good and unusual Sunday lunch dish to serve with Canadian bacon or frizzled ham.

YOU WILL NEED:

White cabbage	Milk
Salt	Eggs
Flour	Butter

Shred 1 white cabbage and cook in boiling water for ½ hour. Drain and boil with 1 teaspoon salt for 15 minutes. Then drain, pressing out all the water. Combine in blender 1 cup sifted flour, ½ cup milk, 2 whole eggs and 1 yolk, ½ teaspoon salt and 3 tablespoons butter. When perfectly smooth remove from blender and combine with cooked cabbage. Heat in skillet 4 tablespoons butter and fry 1 tablespoon mixture on both sides until golden brown.

Red Cabbage

IN THE ALSATIAN MANNER

If you have trouble finding smoked fat back of pork, use a well-smoked bacon or smoked shoulder of pork.

YOU WILL NEED:

Red cabbage	*Pork (smoked fat back)*
White wine	*Salt*
Chicken bouillon	*Potatoes*

Cut the cabbage in ribbons after having discarded the tough ribs. Put it in a large earthenware or enameled pot with 1 cup dry white wine, 1 cup chicken bouillon and ½ pound smoked fat back of pork cut in 1-inch cubes. Place in 250° oven for 2 hours, shaking the pot frequently. Add 1 teaspoon salt. Serve surrounded by steamed potatoes.

Okra in the Oriental Manner

Frozen okra may be used in this recipe but canned okra will not do.

YOU WILL NEED:

	Salt
Okra	*Paprika*
Tomatoes	*Garlic*

Boil 1 pound okra in hot water to cover for 5 minutes. Remove from heat and drain. Place in saucepan over low heat with 4 tomatoes, removing skins and seeds. Season with salt and paprika and a crushed clove of garlic. Shake pan frequently. Cook for 25 to 30 minutes.

Spinach

In Paris when we talked together about her book, Miss Toklas said of this recipe, "It isn't American spinach. It's Central European. Very good and wildly exotic."

YOU WILL NEED:

Spinach	*Garlic*
Olive oil	*Anchovy filets*

Salt and pepper   Fennel seed or ground
Lemon juice   ginger or mace

Wash spinach until perfectly clean. Drain and place in saucepan. Cover and cook for 8 minutes over asbestos mat. Drain and
put under running cold water. Press out all the water. Heat 4
tablespoons olive oil, 1 crushed clove of garlic, 3 anchovy filets
cut in small pieces, ½ teaspoon salt and ½ teaspoon pepper. Add
spinach and simmer 20 minutes. Add 1 teaspoon lemon juice,
½ teaspoon fennel seed or ¾ teaspoon ground ginger or ½ teaspoon mace.

Oyster Plant

Not often do you find oyster plant in the markets here in the
United States but it does appear regularly in all the seed
catalogues and it is not too difficult to grow.

YOU WILL NEED: Rosemary
   Oyster plant   Mace
   Salt   Parsley
   Lemon juice   Butter

In France this is a common but excellent vegetable.

Allow 1½ pounds for 4 people; boil in 4 cups water with 1
teaspoon salt and a squeeze of lemon juice for about 20 minutes.
Drain and sprinkle with rosemary, mace, parsley and ½ teaspoon
salt. Melt 2 teaspoons butter in pan, add vegetables, reheat for
1 minute and serve.

Baked Tomatoes

In France tomatoes are generally smaller than they are in the
United States. If they are large, one tomato will suffice for each
person especially since they are halved and topped with ham
and crumbs.

YOU WILL NEED:

Tomatoes	*Cloves of garlic*
Olive oil	*Salt*
Bread crumbs	*Parsley*
Ham, boiled	*Pepper*

Allow 2 tomatoes for 1 person; cut in half and place in fire-proof dish in which 5 tablespoons olive oil is bubbling. Mix ½ cup dried bread crumbs, 1 cup chopped boiled ham, 2 crushed cloves of garlic, 1 teaspoon salt, 1 tablespoon chopped parsley and ¼ teaspoon pepper. Top tomatoes with this mixture. Sprinkle with bread crumbs and olive oil. Bake in 350° oven for 40 minutes.

Potatoes Primavera

To serve 4.

YOU WILL NEED:

New potatoes (small)	*Chervil*
Lettuce	*Salt*
Green peas	*Butter*
Veal bouillon or chicken	*Parsley*

Simmer covered for ½ hour 1 pound small new potatoes, 1 head of lettuce cut in ribbons, ½ cup fresh green peas, ½ cup veal or chicken bouillon, 1 tablespoon chopped chervil, ½ teaspoon salt and 4 tablespoons butter. Sprinkle with 1 tablespoon parsley before serving.

Green Mashed Potatoes

YOU WILL NEED:

Potatoes	*Light cream*
Butter	*Parsley*
Salt	*Water-cress leaves*
	Basil leaves

For 4 persons bake 4 large potatoes for 40 minutes. Peel them and place in blender at lowest speed with 4 tablespoons soft butter, 1 teaspoon salt, 1 cup light cream, ¼ cup parsley, ½ cup water-cress leaves and 2 tablespoons basil leaves. When well mixed remove from blender and reheat. Serve very hot.

Extravagant Mashed Potatoes

YOU WILL NEED:
> Large potatoes
> Butter
> Salt

For 4 people bake 4 large potatoes, peel and put through the food mill. While the potatoes are still hot add 2 cups butter and 1 teaspoon salt. Undoubtedly 1 pound of butter is extravagant but try it once.

Mushrooms with Cheese

To serve 4.

YOU WILL NEED:
> Mushrooms   Swiss cheese
> Butter   Parmesan cheese
> Béchamel sauce Salt

Chop the stems of 1 pound mushrooms and put aside to use another time. Cut the caps in half and put in saucepan with 4 tablespoons butter. Cook covered over low flame with ½ teaspoon salt until the juice has been absorbed. Add ¼ cup béchamel sauce (see page 97), ¼ cup grated Swiss cheese and ¼ cup grated Parmesan. Bake in buttered fireproof dish in 400° oven for 10 minutes and serve at once.

Cucumbers in Cream

This recipe serves 4 to 6.

YOU WILL NEED: *Veal or chicken stock*
   Cucumbers   *Garlic*
   Sour cream   *Salt*
   Flour   *Paprika*

It is my personal feeling that cucumbers should not be cooked in or with butter, but sour cream in the Turkish manner should be used.

Place 2 tablespoons sour cream in a saucepan over low heat. Stir in 2 tablespoons flour and ½ cup good veal or chicken stock. Simmer, stirring constantly, for 15 minutes. Then add 1 cup sour cream, 1 clove crushed garlic, 1 teaspoon salt, 1 teaspoon paprika and 3 peeled and sliced cucumbers. Cover the saucepan and simmer for 20 minutes.

Artichokes in the Greek Manner

Frozen artichoke hearts are perfect for this excellent recipe. A delightful addition to a tray of hors d'oeuvres.

YOU WILL NEED:
   Artichokes   *Whole white peppers*
   White wine   *Coriander seeds*
   Olive oil   *Bay leaf*
   Salt   *Thyme*

Cut 8 artichokes to the hearts, putting aside for other purposes the leaves, discarding the choke. Boil in covered saucepan in ½ cup white wine, ½ cup olive oil, 1 teaspoon salt, 1 tablespoon whole white peppers, 1 teaspoon coriander seeds, 1 bay leaf and a good twig of thyme. It will take about 25 minutes to cook them. If the liquid is too reduced add a little more white wine. Cool in the juice and serve cold. They can be kept in a covered jar in the refrigerator for several days.

Artichokes Catharine de Medici

If you are not accustomed to cooking with raw pigeon breasts as called for in this recipe, you may substitute quick-frozen breasts of chicken. Usually a single breast will provide about a cupful of chopped meat.

YOU WILL NEED:

Artichokes	Nutmeg
Raw pigeon breasts	Ground pepper
Powdered ginger	Salt
Powdered cloves	Heavy cream

This is a recipe extravagant enough to convince one of its authenticity.

For 4 artichokes prepare a dressing of 3 cups ground raw pigeon breasts. Place on boiled artichokes, having added ¼ teaspoon powdered ginger, ¼ teaspoon powdered cloves, ¼ teaspoon nutmeg, ¼ teaspoon ground pepper and ½ teaspoon salt, mixed with 3 tablespoons heavy cream. When this mixture has been piled on each artichoke heart, cover each with 1 teaspoon heavy cream. Brown in 400° oven for 10 minutes.

SAUCES

Blond Roux

Melt 1 tablespoon butter in saucepan over low heat. Add 1 tablespoon flour. Stir constantly while slowly adding 3 cups hot chicken consommé, ½ teaspoon salt, ¼ teaspoon pepper, 2 tablespoons diced carrots, 1 diced onion, 1 diced shallot, 1 bay leaf. Reduce to 1½ cups. Strain and add 2 tablespoons butter in small pieces.

Dark Roux

Melt 1 tablespoon butter in saucepan over medium heat, add 1 teaspoon salt, ½ teaspoon pepper. When the butter turns golden add 1 tablespoon flour. When the flour is also golden slowly add 3 cups beef bouillon and continue as for blond roux.

White Sauce

YOU WILL NEED:
    Butter
    Flour
    Thin cream

Melt over low flame 1 tablespoon butter, add 1 tablespoon flour. Do not allow to color but add 2 cups hot water slowly; be sure the sauce is smooth. Add 1 cup thin cream and 2 tablespoons butter in small pieces.

Cream Sauce

When egg yolks are used to thicken sauces the hot sauce is added gradually to the stirred yolks of the eggs. Never add the yolks to the sauce or you have a curdled mess.

YOU WILL NEED:
    Butter
    Flour
    Thin cream

Follow white-sauce recipe using no water but thin cream instead. Both these sauces are sometimes thickened with yolks of eggs.

Sauce Béchamel

WITHOUT MEAT FOR FAST DAYS

YOU WILL NEED: Pepper
    Butter   Onion
    Flour   Carrot
    Milk   A bouquet of herbs
    Salt   Heavy cream

A béchamel, let there be no confusion, is not the white sauce served in a dining car; it is not library paste.

Melt 3 tablespoons butter in a saucepan, add 2 tablespoons flour, stir and slowly add 3 cups hot milk, 1 teaspoon salt, ½ teaspoon pepper, 1 sliced onion, 1 diced carrot and a bouquet. Simmer for ½ hour. Strain and add ¼ cup heavy cream.

Béchamel for Feast Days

WITH MEAT

YOU WILL NEED:

Butter	Carrot
Flour	A bouquet of herbs
Consommé	Heavy cream
Salt	Ham
Pepper	Mushrooms
Onion	Chicken or veal

Follow recipe for béchamel sauce without meat, but in addition to the vegetables add ¼ cup diced ham and ¼ cup diced chicken or veal, and instead of 3 cups milk add 3 cups consommé and ½ cup diced mushrooms. Simmer for 2 hours and strain. Add ½ cup heavy cream.

Sauce Mornay

A meatless béchamel (see page 97) with ½ cup grated Swiss cheese added.

Sauce Espagnole

Why not double or even triple the quantity and keep it in small containers in the freezer? Deep freezing even over a period of weeks or months seems to mellow rather than dissipate the flavors. If upon reheating the sauce should show a slight tendency to separate, a touch of the whisk makes it perfect.

YOU WILL NEED:

Butter	Shallots
Flour	Thyme
Bouillon	Bay leaf
Dry white wine	Parsley
Carrot	Clove
Onion	Boiled ham
	Salt and pepper

Prepare a pale roux by melting 3 tablespoons butter over low flame, then adding 2 tablespoons flour. Stirring constantly, slowly add 1 cup hot bouillon and 1 cup hot dry white wine; then add 1 sliced carrot, 1 large sliced onion, 2 shallots, a twig of thyme, 1 bay leaf, several stalks of parsley, 1 clove, ½ cup diced lean boiled ham, 1 teaspoon salt, 1 teaspoon pepper. Cover and boil slowly for ¾ hour. Strain.

This is good to have on hand. Well covered, it will keep in the refrigerator for 10 days.

Sauce Italian

YOU WILL NEED:

Butter	Salt and pepper
Flour	Nutmeg
Bouillon	Shallot
Dry white wine	Parsley
Mushrooms	Tarragon
Garlic	Chervil
Bay leaf	Lemon juice
Clove	Cayenne

A sauce roux of 3 tablespoons butter and 2 tablespoons flour is thinned with 2 cups bouillon and 1 cup hot dry white wine. Add ½ cup chopped mushrooms, 1 crushed clove garlic, ½ bay leaf, 1 clove, ½ teaspoon salt, ½ teaspoon pepper, a good pinch powdered nutmeg and a shallot. Cook for ½ hour and strain. Return to very low heat and simmer, adding 3 tablespoons butter, 2 tablespoons chopped parsley, 1 tablespoon chopped tarragon, 1 tablespoon chopped chervil, a squeeze of lemon juice and a good pinch of cayenne.

Mushroom Sauce

YOU WILL NEED:

Mushrooms	Bread crumbs
Butter	Bouillon
Salt	Béchamel sauce
Lemon juice	Nutmeg

Put 1 pound finely chopped mushrooms in 4 tablespoons butter with ½ teaspoon salt and a squeeze of lemon juice. Cook covered over medium flame for 15 minutes. Remove from heat and add ¾ cup fresh bread crumbs that have been soaking in hot bouillon and from which all the moisture has been extracted. Mix well and pound through a hair sieve. Put this purée into a saucepan with ¼ cup stiff béchamel sauce (see page 97), ½ teaspoon salt and a pinch of powdered nutmeg. Add 2 tablespoons butter but do not allow it to boil further.

Essence of Mushrooms

An inspired way to make use of stems and bits of mushrooms! You will use this essence many times to pick up the flavor of all sorts of dishes—canned soups, for instance.

YOU WILL NEED:

Mushroom stems
Veal or chicken bouillon

Bring to a boil 1 pound mushroom stems in 2 cups veal or chicken bouillon. Cover and simmer until reduced by half.

Strain by pounding through muslin cloth placed in sieve. When cold cover tightly. Keeps well in refrigerator and is invaluable.

Essence of Celery

YOU WILL NEED:
> Celery
> Chicken consommé

Cut in rings 1 pound celery stalks and leaves. Simmer covered in 2 cups chicken consommé until the liquid has been absorbed. Add 2 more cups chicken consommé and simmer covered for 15 minutes. Strain and keep as above.

Tarragon Essence

May be prepared and kept as above.

Sauce Rouille (Provence)

FOR BOUILLABAISSE AND FISH SOUP

Jean, the distinguished host of La Méditerranée restaurant in Paris, introduced me to this interesting sauce. It gives such authenticity to a bouillabaisse even though the bouillabaisse of the moment may be made unauthentically from local fishes.

YOU WILL NEED:
> Garlic
> Red peppers
> Salt
> Bread crumbs
> Fish soup
> Olive oil

Take 4 cloves of garlic and 2 hot red peppers, 1 teaspoon salt and ½ cup bread crumbs that have been soaking in a little hot fish soup and from which all moisture has been extracted. Pound this in a mortar until it has become what they call in Provence a pomade or a marmalade. It must be smooth before commencing to add 1 cup olive oil drop by drop. There are those who use the yolk of an egg instead of the bread crumbs but they are not well thought of.

The sauce is hot and strong and delicious.

Frozen Aiolli

YOU WILL NEED:

Garlic	Chives
Onion	Capers
Parsley leaves	White pepper
Tarragon leaves	Salt
Chervil leaves	Cayenne
Basil leaves	Cream

This is a suitable sauce for any cold fish. I like it with cracked crab, and a friend served it with cold chicken.

Crush 2 garlic buds in a mortar with 1 small onion, 1 tablespoon parsley leaves, 1 tablespoon tarragon leaves, ½ teaspoon chervil leaves, 1 teaspoon basil leaves, 1 teaspoon chives and 4 capers. Add a pinch of white pepper, ½ teaspoon salt, a pinch of cayenne. Force through a hair sieve. Gently fold into this 1 cup whipped cream and freeze.

White Butter Nantes

FOR FISH

This recipe is a treasure very difficult to come by, for the white butter sauce of Nantes is one of those traditional specialties which every family knows but practically no one has set down on paper.

YOU WILL NEED: Butter
    Vinegar   Salt
    Fish court bouillon   Pepper

Simmer 1 tablespoon vinegar and ½ cup strained (clarified) fish court bouillon (see page 21) until reduced by half. Add ½ cup butter in small pieces at a time. Stir constantly in the same direction. Add ½ teaspoon salt and ¼ teaspoon pepper. Serve as soon as the butter is melted.

Sauce à la Sultane

YOU WILL NEED: Parsley
    Bouillon   Onion
    Lemon   Carrot
    Cloves   Salt
    Garlic   Pepper
    Bay leaf   Egg

Put 2 cups bouillon in saucepan over medium heat. Add 2 slices of lemon from which the rind has been removed, 2 cloves, 1 clove garlic, ½ bay leaf, 2 sprigs parsley, 1 onion and 1 carrot. Reduce heat and simmer for 1 hour. Strain through a fine sieve. Return to saucepan and add ½ teaspoon salt, ¼ teaspoon pepper, the crushed yolk of 1 hard-boiled egg and 1 teaspoon chopped parsley.

Very good for fish, chicken or beef.

Sauce Bachique

YOU WILL NEED: Tarragon
    Olive oil   Dried chervil leaves
    Bouillon   Parsley
    Dry white wine   Green onion
    Shallot   Garlic
    Water cress   Pepper and salt

Put 1 tablespoon olive oil in a saucepan with 2 cups good bouillon and 1 cup good dry white wine. Simmer covered until it is reduced by half. Then add 1 shallot, a handful of water cress, 3 branches of tarragon, 2 tablespoons dried chervil leaves and 2 tablespoons parsley, 1 green onion, 1 clove garlic, all chopped very, very fine. Add ½ teaspoon pepper and 1 teaspoon salt.

This can be used for any and everything: fish, meat or vegetables. Can be kept for several days in refrigerator.

Russian Sauce

If freshly grated horseradish root is not available you may use dehydrated horseradish: ½ tablespoon reconstituted with a couple of tablespoons of water. Or if you can find it and sometimes you can, use quick-frozen horseradish. Horseradish in vinegar is readily available. If you use it you may wish to omit the lemon juice. Taste and see what is necessary.

YOU WILL NEED: *Grated horseradish*
   Butter   *Chives*
   Flour   *Lemon juice*
   Chicken bouillon   *Heavy cream*

Make a roux (see page 96) with 1 tablespoon butter, 1 tablespoon flour and 1 cup chicken bouillon. Simmer for ¼ hour, add 1 tablespoon grated horseradish, ½ teaspoon slivered chives, a few drops of lemon juice and ¼ cup heavy cream. Simmer 2 minutes and strain. Reheat but be careful not to allow sauce to boil.

Suitable for baked fish or potato salad. Delicious with grilled calf's brains.

Cold Horseradish Sauce

Use fresh, coarsely grated horseradish if you can get it. If not, use dehydrated, quick-frozen or bottled horseradish.

YOU WILL NEED:

Horseradish   Cayenne
Salt   Cream

Mix 4 tablespoons grated horseradish with ½ teaspoon salt
and a good pinch of cayenne. Fold in 1 cup whipped cream.
Serve cold with cold boiled beef or boiled fish.

Another Cold Horseradish Sauce

YOU WILL NEED:

Apples   Lemon juice
Horseradish   Cayenne
Salt   Brandy

Mix ½ cup grated apples with ½ cup grated horseradish. Add
¼ teaspoon salt, ¼ teaspoon lemon juice, a pinch of cayenne
and ½ teaspoon brandy.

Sauce to Serve with Cold Fish or Cold Meat

*Miss Toklas remarks: "This is a nice salad dressing for hearts
of romaine and skinned cherry tomatoes, placed alternately in
salad bowl, with the sauce in the center."*

YOU WILL NEED: Pepper
Butter   Mayonnaise
Flour   Dry mustard
Thin cream   Parsley
Salt   Dill pickles

Make a cream sauce with 1 tablespoon melted butter and 1
tablespoon flour. Add 1 cup thin cream, ½ teaspoon salt and ¼
teaspoon pepper. Simmer over low flame, stirring constantly, for
15 minutes. Remove from flame and cool. When perfectly cold
incorporate 1 cup mayonnaise. Add 1 teaspoon dry mustard, 1
teaspoon very finely chopped parsley and 1 tablespoon finely
chopped dill pickles.

A Cream Sauce with Fine Herbs

YOU WILL NEED: Lemon
    Leaves of chervil   Dry mustard
    Parsley   Cream
    Tarragon leaves   Eggs
    Shallot   Butter

Mix 6 tablespoons finely chopped leaves of chervil, 6 tablespoons finely chopped parsley, 6 tablespoons finely chopped
tarragon leaves, 1 crushed shallot and the juice of a lemon. Add
1 tablespoon dry mustard. Add ¾ cup whipped cream and the
stirred yolks of 2 eggs. Put in saucepan over lowest heat, and
stirring constantly in the same direction add 3 tablespoons butter
cut in small pieces. Do not allow to boil. Add juice of ½ lemon
and serve at once. Serve with chicken, veal or fish.

White Butter Sauce

*In Holland and Belgium white butter sauce is popular and
highly regarded. The trick of making it, and there is a slight
trick: keep the heat very, very low indeed. If you have an automatically controlled burner or skillet, set the thermostat at about
180°—well below the simmering point.*

YOU WILL NEED: Vinegar
    Butter   Salt
    Shallots   Pepper

Melt 1 cup butter in saucepan over low heat with 3 finely
chopped shallots, 1 teaspoon vinegar, ½ teaspoon salt and ¼
teaspoon pepper. Stir constantly with wooden spoon. As soon as
the butter is melted pour into heated sauceboat. Fine with grilled
meat or fish.

To Roast a Pound of Butter

According to A. B. T.: *"This is an incomparable sauce for turbot and (yes, indeed) on a grilled châteaubriant."*

YOU WILL NEED:
Butter   Nutmeg
Fresh bread crumbs   Oysters

Roll 2 cups butter in 1 cup fresh bread crumbs in which 1 teaspoon powdered nutmeg has been mixed. Place a skewer through the butter. Grill very very slowly with a dish underneath to catch the drippings as the butter melts, with which you will constantly baste the mixture. Heat 1 pint oysters in their liquid but do not allow to boil. When the butter has soaked up all the bread crumbs place on your oysters and serve at once.

Sauce Suprême

YOU WILL NEED: Veal or chicken consommé
Butter   Essence of mushrooms
Flour   Heavy cream

Melt ¼ cup butter over low heat, add ½ cup sifted flour and stir slowly, adding 4 cups veal or chicken consommé. Simmer for 1½ hours. Add 2 cups chicken or veal consommé and ¼ cup essence of mushrooms (see page 100). Cook until the sauce has been reduced by three-fourths. Then add ¼ cup heavy cream. Simmer until the spoon is coated. Strain. Reheat and at the last moment add 3 tablespoons butter. Do not allow to boil further.

Madeira Sauce

YOU WILL NEED:

Onions	Madeira wine
Butter	Salt and pepper
Flour	A bouquet of herbs
Bouillon	Mushrooms

Cook 2 large chopped onions in ⅓ cup butter only enough to brown lightly. Remove the onions and set aside. Add 1½ teaspoons flour to the butter in the saucepan, moisten with 1½ cups hot bouillon and ⅓ cup Madeira wine. Cook over low flame, stirring constantly. Add salt and pepper, a bouquet and the onions. Cook gently for 20 minutes and strain. Reheat and add ¾ pound very small mushrooms. Cook for 20 minutes further. If the sauce becomes too thick add a little more Madeira.

Sauce Hollandaise

YOU WILL NEED:

Eggs	Butter
Salt	Lemon juice

Put 4 stirred yolks of eggs over the lowest possible flame with ½ tablespoon water and 1 teaspoon salt. Stir continually in the same direction while slowly adding small pieces of 1 pound of butter you will eventually incorporate into the yolks of eggs. Keep the flame down, add the butter slowly and in small pieces, only one piece melting at a time. It is foolproof if you go slowly —¼ hour will do it. If you are called to the telephone put it off the stove and go back to it. A whisk makes it light and foamy. Incorporate 1 tablespoon lemon juice toward the end.

Anchovy Sauce

YOU WILL NEED:

Shallot	*Salt and pepper*
Butter	*Anchovies*
Madeira wine	*Eggs*

Cook for 15 minutes over low flame 1 chopped shallot in 1 tablespoon butter. Pour over it ½ cup good Madeira, add a pinch of pepper and of salt. Reduce a little and remove from heat. Cool. Pound 10 anchovies with the yolks of 2 eggs. Slowly add to it the strained liquid in which the shallot has been cooked and stir over the lowest possible heat, turning with a wooden spoon until it is coated. Remove from heat and strain.

Sauce Béarnaise

YOU WILL NEED:

White wine vinegar	*Pepper*
Shallot	*Thyme*
Leaves of tarragon	*Bay leaf*
Leaves of chervil	*Eggs*
Salt	*Butter*

Put ½ cup of good white wine vinegar in a small saucepan with 1 finely chopped shallot, 1 tablespoon leaves of tarragon, 1 teaspoon leaves of chervil, a pinch of salt, a good pinch of pepper, a pinch of powdered thyme and one of bay leaf. Simmer over very low flame until reduced to 1 tablespoon. Strain. When cold add 2 yolks of eggs diluted with 1 tablespoon water. Add, over lowest flame, ½ cup butter in small pieces. Stir constantly, only adding a new piece of butter when the last piece is melted.

Sauce Choron

YOU WILL NEED:
> *Béarnaise sauce*
> *Concentrated tomato paste*

This is a béarnaise sauce (see page 109) to which ¾ cup concentrated tomato paste has been added at the last moment.

Hot Mayonnaise

If you want to use the blender simply place all the ingredients except the hot water into the blender in the order in which they are named. After blending a few seconds pour the hot water into the center while the blender is still running. The sauce will then need only a minute or so of heating and stirring in a double boiler or over very low heat on a controlled burner.

YOU WILL NEED:
Olive oil	*Parsley*
Eggs	*Dry mustard*
Dry white wine	*Salt*
Hot water	*White pepper*

Slowly add 3 tablespoons olive oil to 2 yolks of eggs. Gradually add 1 tablespoon dry white wine and ½ cup hot water. Cook in double boiler, stirring constantly, until the spoon is coated. Add 1 teaspoon chopped parsley, ¼ teaspoon dry mustard, ½ teaspoon salt and ½ teaspoon ground white pepper. Serve hot.

Very good with asparagus, artichokes, broccoli and celeriac.

SALADS AND SALAD DRESSINGS

Salad Dandy

YOU WILL NEED:

Shrimps	*Eggs*
Lettuce	*Truffles or black olives*
	Mayonnaise

Place shrimps, boiled and de-veined, on lettuce and cover
with chopped eggs and chopped truffles, tastefully arranged. If
the week's, month's or year's budget does not admit truffles, black
olives may not replace them but they are tasty and give the
necessary note to the color scheme. Put mayonnaise in the center
of the serving dish.

Salad Margot

*Peanut oil or sesame-seed oil may be substituted here for olive
oil. If you do use olive oil be sure that it is a light virgin oil. A
heavy oil would overpower the delicate flavor of bananas.*

YOU WILL NEED:

Hearts of celery	*Curry*
Bananas	*Olive oil*

Cut 1 cup tender white hearts of celery into 2-inch lengths,
add 1 cup sliced bananas. Season with a pinch of curry and at
the last moment pour a little olive oil over the bowl.

Latin Chichighi Salatassi

(KINDNESS OF MR. EUGENE WALTER)

YOU WILL NEED:

Flowers of nasturtiums	Salt
Chervil	*Olive oil*
	Lemon

Contributed to the *Turkish Cookery Book,* 1862, by Turale Effendi.

Put a plate of the flowers of nasturtiums in a salad bowl, with a tablespoon of chopped chervil. Sprinkle over with your fingers ½ tsp. of salt, pour over 2 or 3 tablespoons olive oil and the juice of a lemon. Turn the salad in the bowl with a spoon and fork until well mixed and serve.

Salad Marie Louise

YOU WILL NEED:

Potatoes	Pepper
Apples	Eggs
Olive oil	Corn
Salt	Violets

The Empress Marie Louise and the last Empress of Russia had a weakness for violets, not only for flavoring desserts—for here is a recipe where they are among the ingredients in a salad.

Take equal parts of sliced boiled cold potatoes and raw peeled and sliced apples. Add oil, salt and pepper. Mix at the last moment and place in a mound in the center of the salad bowl. Sprinkle with crushed hard-boiled eggs. Surround with alternate small mounds of corn and of violets, stems removed.

Salad Dressing

YOU WILL NEED:

Egg	Olive oil
Salt	Lemon juice
Dry mustard	Absinthe, Pernod or dry vermouth

To the yolk of 1 egg add ½ teaspoon salt and ¼ teaspoon dry mustard. Mix and, stirring constantly, add slowly 3 tablespoons olive oil, 1 tablespoon lemon juice and 1 teaspoon absinthe, Pernod or dry vermouth.

Salad Dressing à l'Ancienne

YOU WILL NEED:

Cream cheese	Olive oil
Dry mustard	Lemon juice
Chervil	Salt
Estragon	Pepper

Mix ½ cup cream cheese with ½ teaspoon dry mustard, 1 teaspoon chopped chervil and 1 teaspoon chopped estragon. Beat in drop by drop 4 tablespoons olive oil, 1 tablespoon lemon juice, ½ teaspoon salt and ¼ teaspoon ground pepper.

Green Mayonnaise

YOU WILL NEED:	Lemon or lime juice
Egg	Cress leaves
Salt	Spinach
Pepper	Chervil
Olive oil	Estragon

Put the yolk of an egg in a bowl with ½ teaspoon salt and ¼ teaspoon pepper. Stir well. Add drop by drop 2 tablespoons olive oil, stirring constantly. When it commences to stiffen add a few drops lemon or lime juice and commence to pour oil in more quickly. It will require ¾ cup oil and the juice of ½ lemon or lime. The mayonnaise must be particularly firm. Gradually add the following purée:

Take equal parts of cress leaves, spinach, chervil and estragon. Boil them for 2 minutes in unsalted water to cover. Drain and put under cold-water tap. Press out all the water. Squeeze in a clean cloth. Pound them in mortar until reduced to a pulp that can be pounded through a fine muslin. It should make ¼ cup.

Add to the mayonnaise, to which the greens will give not only a color but a flavor.

Green Hollandaise Sauce

Add the above purée to a hollandaise sauce (see page 108) long enough to heat the greens before serving.

Salad Dressing from Cataluña

If you have an electric blender you need not bother to crush the egg yolks or the garlic or to chop the chives or sweet pepper. Simply put a tablespoon of lemon juice and a tablespoon of prepared mustard into the glass container, add the egg yolks, chives, garlic and sweet pepper cut into strips. Blend 10 seconds and while blender is still whirring add 6 tablespoons olive oil. Blend about 20 seconds longer.

YOU WILL NEED:

Eggs	Garlic
Mustard	Sweet red pepper
Chives	Olive oil
	Lemon juice

Crush the yolks of 2 hard-boiled eggs with 1 tablespoon prepared mustard. Add 2 tablespoons minced chives, 1 crushed clove of garlic and 1 chopped sweet red pepper from which skin and seeds have been removed. Beat in drop by drop 6 tablespoons olive oil and 1 tablespoon lemon juice. Cut the hard-boiled whites of the 2 eggs like shoe-string potatoes and place on salad before serving.

Rosé Vinegar

YOU WILL NEED:
    Rose petals
    White wine vinegar

Put 1 cup freshly gathered rose petals in 1 quart jar. Cover with best white wine vinegar. Place in sun for 2 weeks. Strain through paper filter. Bottle and cork. Delicious for salads.

Hazel-Nut Oil

YOU WILL NEED:
> *Hazel nuts*
> *Olive oil*

Place 12 hazel nuts in a pan in a warm oven, leaving door open. Shake from time to time. When they are hot but not toasted remove from oven and roll vigorously in a cloth. This will remove the skins. Pound them very fine and pour 1 cup boiling olive oil over them and infuse, covered, for 12 hours. Strain and bottle. The strained nuts can be used to excellent effect in an egg or green salad.

If the hazel-nut oil is rare, exquisite and expensive, what can one say of

Pistachio Oil

YOU WILL NEED:
> *Pistachio nuts*
> *Olive oil*

To blanch shelled pistachio nuts proceed as for almonds, only be careful not to have the pistachios in water any longer than necessary for they will lose their vivid green color. Soak a few at a time. It will require ⅓ cup pistachios to 1 cup olive oil. Proceed as above. To be served as a salad oil for tossed and all vegetable salads. Exquisite with artichokes, asparagus, tomatoes, leeks, etc.

DESSERTS

Iced Peaches à la Grecque

Canned peaches packed whole with their seeds or even peach halves of the finest type can be used instead of freshly poached peaches in this recipe.

Instead of pounding the ripe figs through a fine strainer you can place them in an electric blender along with about ¼ cup of the syrup from the peaches. Cook for 10 minutes with ¾ cup syrup to make a kind of fig marmalade, which is to be flavored with kirsch and combined with whipped cream as covering for the peaches. Serves 6.

YOU WILL NEED:
- Peaches
- Sugar
- Figs

Alsatian kirsch
Heavy cream
Strawberries
Pistachios

Pure Essence of Arabian Nights.

Pour boiling water over 6 fine peaches and peel them. Poach them for 10 minutes in a syrup of 1 cup water and 1 cup sugar that has cooked for 5 minutes. Drain the peaches and remove to shallow serving dish. Pound through a fine strainer 12 ripe figs and cook for 10 minutes in the syrup in which the peaches were cooked. Cool the marmalade and add ¼ cup real Alsatian kirsch and 3 cups whipped heavy cream. Cover the peaches with this mixture and decorate with a few small strawberries and finely chopped pistachios. Put in the refrigerator 1 hour before serving.

Pears à la Lapérouse

YOU WILL NEED:

Pears	*Crème Anglaise*
Sugar	*Praline powder*
Vanilla bean	*Rum*

The restaurant Lapérouse is three blocks from where I live and it has been my pleasure over these many years to become well acquainted with its famous cuisine. It was indeed my introduction to the great Paris restaurants. Of the three of that time it is now the last. The Café Anglais closed with the '14-'18 war and Voisin's, as I remember, very shortly after.

The first time I dined at Lapérouse the California friend who was my host wished the event to be marked with all that ceremonial San Francisco considered Parisian. We were ushered up the narrow winding stairway to a room with a bright boulet fire—a restrained bouquet of forget-me-nots and white pompon dahlias, no fragrance—perish the thought—to interfere with the aroma of the food, a sommelier, a maître d'hôtel and a waiter in solemn silent attendance. We were doubtless served with more rare dishes than I would have wished. One thing impressed itself upon me. There were vintages for champagne as well as for wine, not just names of the vintners. Well, well, the Seine has been in flood several times since then.

This is a simple but exquisite dish which has been ordered often enough for me to be able to tell you how to prepare it.

First, select the best and most fondant pears the market offers. Peel them but do not remove their stems. Simmer them in a syrup of half sugar, half water in which ½ vanilla bean is infusing. The pears should be removed from the syrup as soon as they can be pierced with a spoon. They should remain gently resistant. Drain and place upright on shallow serving dish, pour around them a crème anglaise (see page 129) flavored with rum in which 1 tablespoon per pear praline powder (see page 129) has been stirred. Serve cold but not chilled.

Stewed Apples

This is another instance where Alice Toklas uses ordinary ingredients to achieve a notable and unexpectedly different result. The quality of the apples is important. You should use tart, solid, nonmealy apples. Green apples will do, or Greenings, York, Northern Spies if you can get them, Baldwins or McIntosh early in the season. So-called Delicious apples will not do.

YOU WILL NEED:

> *Tart apples*
> *Sugar*
> *Rum*

Minus the rum this is an old-fashioned country dish but quite well worth reviving.

For 4 persons peel 4 tart apples, remove the cores and slice. Put over low heat in a covered saucepan with 1 cup sugar. It will take from 15 minutes to ½ hour to cook them, depending upon the quality of the apples. Do not overcook. This is not an applesauce. Before serving, cold, tepid or hot, add 1 tablespoon of rum.

Apple Mousse

Mere applesauce cannot be substituted for the richly glazed and almost caramelized purée of apples called for in this recipe. However, you may use the blender if you don't want to "pound through a fine sieve." The heavy cream may be lightly whipped but it is not necessary.

YOU WILL NEED:

> *Apples*   *Heavy cream*
> *Sugar*   *Strawberry purée sauce*

Peel 6 apples, core them and cut in slices. Mix with 1 cup sugar and ¼ cup water. Place in saucepan over low heat and cover.

Cook for 3 hours; be careful that they do not scorch or, worse still, burn. It is wise to cook them over an asbestos mat. When they are cooked pound through a fine sieve. When they are cold fold in ½ cup heavy cream. Place in a lightly oiled mold in the refrigerator overnight. Serve with a strawberry purée sauce (see below).

Strawberry Purée

Remove the stems from a pint of strawberries. Press through a fine sieve. Add 3 tablespoons confectioner's sugar. Keep in refrigerator until time to serve.

Apple Pie

This is an apple pie completely unlike the classic American type. The filling is different, for the apples are precooked with wine and then made into sauce. The single crust is different, made from pâte brisée, and the pie is frosted like a cake with a rum-flavored butter icing.

A proud confection.

YOU WILL NEED:

Apples	Red or white wine
Sugar	Baked pâté brisée

For butter icing: Confectioner's sugar
    Butter   Rum

Make an applesauce of 1½ pounds of apples, ½ cup sugar and just enough good red or white wine to prevent burning, the quantity depending upon the apples. When cooked strain through a fine sieve. It must have a certain consistency. Place in a previously baked pâte brisée (see page 120). When cold pour over the apples a butter icing of 1½ cups confectioner's sugar, 2 teaspoons soft butter and 2 tablespoons good pale rum, all of which have been stirred to a cream.

Pâte Brisée

One-half pound flour, ⅓ pound butter and a pinch of salt. Just enough cold water to combine in a bowl with a knife. Work quickly and lightly, as with any good pie crust.

A Splendid Avocado Sherbet

(ADAPTED FROM LADY MENDL'S RECIPE BY MR. EUGENE WALTER)

Miss Toklas says of this dish, "Once in New York I gave a luncheon to honor the first trip to that city of a beautiful southern girl of 18 years, and served this with great effect. Each plate was arranged on a shallow serving bowl full of cracked ice on which was sprinkled sequin dust, and in the guest of honor's dish was frozen a tiny jade charm for a surprise. Very good washed down with champagne. Traditional for Brazilian wedding breakfasts." Makes about a quart.

YOU WILL NEED: *Sugar*
   Buttermilk   *Light corn syrup*
   Lemon juice   *Avocado*

Mix 2 cups buttermilk with ¼ cup lemon juice, ½ cup sugar and ½ cup light corn syrup. Pour into freezing tray, set control at coldest point; freeze to mush stage. Pour into chilled bowl, beat ferociously until smooth, smooth, smooth. Then add 1 cup ripe, ripe, ripe avocado from which any stringy fibers have been removed. Mash. Return to tray, freeze until firm. (This is pale jade green, smooth, unctuous, witty, but never forward.)

Flaming Bananas

Instead of kirsch you may use a good golden rum, cognac or brandy.

YOU WILL NEED: *Sugar*
  Butter *Kirsch*
  Bananas *Vanilla ice cream*

Put ½ cup butter in large skillet over low flame. When melted place 6 peeled bananas in the skillet and cook slowly. Turn frequently so that all sides may be lightly browned. Cook 20 minutes but no more. Then add ¾ cup sugar. Turn so that all the bananas will be coated. Cook 2 minutes. Remove to hot serving dish and pour over them ½ cup kirsch. Serve, lighted, with vanilla ice cream. A pleasant surprise.

Chocolate Brick

YOU WILL NEED: *Eggs*
  Sweet chocolate *Lady fingers*
  Milk *Sauce anglaise*

Melt ½ pound chocolate in a double boiler, add ½ cup milk and stir until perfectly smooth. Pour this slowly over the well-stirred yolks of 2 eggs. Return to the double boiler and stir until it coats the spoon. Remove from double boiler and stir occasionally. Place on serving dish 3 lady fingers side by side. Pour over them a little of the chocolate-and-egg mixture. Place on the lady fingers 3 more of them but crosswise to the first layer. Pour over them a little of the mixture. Continue in this manner until all the chocolate mixture has been used, reserving only enough to cover the four sides. Put aside for 1 hour. Serve with a vanilla-flavored sauce anglaise (see page 129).

Cold Chocolate Pudding

Basically, this is a chocolate bread pudding—an exalted left-over dish. But if, as is often the case in the modern household, you have no stale bread on hand for crumbs you can of course use the kind that comes already finely ground, sieved and browned in a package. Makes 4 to 6 servings.

YOU WILL NEED:

    Sweet chocolate   Egg

    Milk   Butter

    Bread crumbs   Sauce anglaise

Melt in double boiler 3 squares chocolate in 2 cups milk. Stir until perfectly smooth. Add 1 cup browned bread crumbs. Stir until the bread crumbs are absorbed. Add the yolk of 1 egg, stir until the spoon is coated. Then fold in the white of the egg that has been beaten just to the peak stage. Pour in buttered mold placed in a pan of hot water—which must not boil—and bake for 15 minutes. Remove from mold when cold and serve with a liqueur-flavored sauce anglaise (see page 129).

Chocolate Mousse

Generally we do not consider using the blender for egg whites or cream but in this case it gives just the right consistency to the dessert—makes it taste just exactly like Paris.

YOU WILL NEED: Heavy cream

    Eggs   Confectioner's sugar

    Sweet chocolate   Cointreau or white curaçao

This is a very old but quickly prepared French dessert. Place in the blender at lowest speed the yolks of 4 eggs, ¼ pound melted chocolate, ½ cup heavy cream and ½ cup confectioner's sugar. After two or three minutes, add the whites of 4 eggs. In another two or three minutes the mixture should be quite light. Remove from the blender and place in a serving bowl in the refrigerator for at least 4 hours.

Serve with 1½ cups whipped cream to which 2 tablespoons confectioner's sugar and 2 tablespoons cointreau or white curaçao have been added while whipping.

Hot Chocolate Sauce

YOU WILL NEED: *Egg*
   Sweet chocolate   *Sugar*
   Thin cream   *Vanilla*

Stir 4 squares sweet chocolate, ¾ cup thin cream, 1 well-stirred egg and 1 cup sugar in top of double boiler over low flame. Stir until well blended. Continue to stir over low heat for 20 minutes. Add 1 teaspoon vanilla before serving.

Cold Chocolate Sauce

YOU WILL NEED:
   Sweet chocolate   *Sugar*
   Milk   *Rum or very strong coffee*
   Eggs   *Cream*

Melt 4 squares sweet chocolate in 3 tablespoons hot milk. Add the yolks (well beaten) of two eggs to ¾ cup milk in which ½ cup sugar has been added. Mix this with the melted chocolate and stir over lowest heat until the spoon is coated. Remove from heat and stir occasionally until cold. Add 1 tablespoon rum or very strong coffee. Just before serving, add ¾ cup whipped cream.

Peasant Girl with a Veil

This is a country dessert which appears in many of the most ancient English cook books. Basically nothing but bread and jelly, it makes, in this day and age, an excellent, convenient and dramatic icebox dessert.

When time saving is uppermost in your mind you might use prepared graham cracker crumbs that come in a box.

YOU WILL NEED:
  Graham, whole-wheat or rye bread crumbs
  Red currant jelly
  Heavy cream

Mix 2 cups graham, whole-wheat or rye bread crumbs, dried in the oven, with 1 cup red currant jelly. Roll into a ball and chill. Before serving, roll in heavy whipped cream and slice in sections.

Crêpes

Some fine cooks turn crêpes with their finger tips. Simply lift an edge and flip.

YOU WILL NEED: *Eggs*
  Flour   *Salt*
  Beer   *Orange*
  Kirsch   *Butter*

For 10 or 12 crêpes mix 2 cups sifted flour with 1 cup hot water and 1 cup beer, 1 tablespoon kirsch and 5 eggs, ¼ teaspoon salt and the grated zest of an orange. Mix in blender until smooth. Put aside for 4 hours. Then give it 1 minute in the blender again. Heat the pan and brush it with a little melted butter. Place only enough batter in the pan to cover it. The crêpes must be very thin and cooked only enough to turn with a spatula.

Tender Pancakes

YOU WILL NEED:
  Flour   *Cognac*
  Sugar   *Butter*
  Milk   *Frangipani cream*
  Eggs   *Liqueur of choice*

Mix in the blender at lowest speed 2 cups sifted flour, ¼ cup sugar, 2 cups milk, 4 eggs and ¼ cup best cognac. When quite smooth remove from blender and put aside for at least 3 hours— not in refrigerator. Then brush with melted butter a small light shallow pan which should be kept especially for this purpose. Pour into it only enough batter to just cover. Turn in all directions to cover as thinly as possible. It is ready to turn when the edges are cooked, and it can be turned with the aid of a spatula. Our best crêpe maker was an Indo-Chinese youth who delicately turned them by hand. They should scarcely be colored. Before rolling, 2 tablespoons frangipani cream (see below) can be placed on each crêpe—they can be served lighted with any liqueur of your choice.

Frangipani Cream

YOU WILL NEED:

Flour	Butter
Sugar	Macaroon
Milk	Egg yolks

One tablespoon flour, 1 tablespoon sugar, ½ cup milk, 1 tablespoon butter, 1 macaroon rolled to a powder. Mix thoroughly. Place over low heat with 2 egg yolks. Stir constantly. Do not allow to boil. When thickened remove at once from heat.

Grandmamma's Fritters

"After two major wars," Miss Toklas says in connection with this recipe, "nothing but absolutely nothing is thrown away." She suggests that you keep in a covered jar the rum in which the raisins are soaked, for "it will be useful later for flavoring desserts." Nevertheless, this recipe, which can be made with leftover cake, is remarkable not for economy but for delight.

YOU WILL NEED: *Rum*
    Sponge or cup cake   *Apricot jam*
    Crystallized pineapple   *Milk*
    Orange peel   *Egg*
    Crystallized cherries   *Bread crumbs*
    Crystallized plums   *Clarified butter*
    Seedless raisins   *Powdered sugar*

Cut 8 slices about ½ inch thick of sponge or cup cake. Dice ½ cup crystallized pineapple, ½ cup orange peel, ½ cup crystallized cherries and ½ cup crystallized plums. Put these with 1 cup seedless raisins covered with rum to soak for 4 hours. Then drain and add ¾ cup strained apricot jam. Keep the rum in a covered jar (it will be useful later for flavoring desserts). Spread the crystallized fruit–jam mixture on 4 of the slices of cake. Cover with the other 4 slices, pressing them well down. Place them in a shallow dish and pour over them just enough hot milk to cover. When the milk is tepid drain well and dip them in a well-beaten egg and then cover with fresh bread crumbs. Put 4 tablespoons clarified butter (see page 22) in a large skillet and brown on both sides over medium heat until golden brown. Sprinkle with powdered sugar and serve very hot. For 4 persons.

Batter for Fritters

YOU WILL NEED:
    Flour   *Salt*
    Milk   *Sugar*
    Butter   *Eggs*
    Brandy, kirsch or rum   *Peanut oil*

Mix thoroughly in blender 1 cup and 1 tablespoon sifted flour, 1 cup hot milk, 1 tablespoon melted butter, ½ cup brandy, kirsch or rum, a pinch of salt, 1 tablespoon sugar and 2 eggs. When satin smooth, remove from blender and set aside several hours. Fry in deep peanut oil (370° F.), drain, put on cookie sheet, dredge with confectioner's sugar and put in oven to glaze.

Fruit that is to be fried in this dough should be sliced and soaked in sweetened cognac, kirsch or rum 1 hour in advance. Then drain well.

Orange-Flower Soufflé

Orange-flower water may not be available at druggists' in the United States. Generally it comes from specialty food shops. No matter where you live you may order it by mail from such firms as S. S. Pierce in Boston, or Charles & Company in New York.

Almond-paste macaroons, in case you have any doubt about it, are the regular classic type available in every bake shop in France and Italy, not to mention Holland, Spain and Sweden. But if you have any trouble finding these in the United States they can be mail-ordered in tins. Or you can even buy a macaroon mix and make them quite easily yourself.

This 6-egg soufflé should serve 4.

YOU WILL NEED:
> Almond-paste macaroons
> Orange-flower water
> Eggs
> Powdered sugar
> Butter

Break 6 almond-paste macaroons into small bits, place in bowl and cover with ½ cup orange-flower water, which can be purchased at a good prescription druggist's. Separate 6 eggs. Stir the yolks with ½ cup sifted powdered sugar until they are pale yellow. Add the crushed macaroons. Fold into this mixture the beaten whites of 6 eggs. Put into a skillet over medium heat ¼ cup butter. Allow it to become golden brown. Then pour the soufflé mixture into it. When it commences to become golden transfer it to a buttered soufflé dish. It should not be more than three-quarters full. Place in 450° oven for 10 minutes. When it becomes slightly browned on top and puffed up quite high, sprinkle with powdered sugar and serve at once.

Currant or Raspberry Slip-and-Go-Easy

YOU WILL NEED:
>   Raspberry or currant jelly
>   Cream cheese
>   Eggs
>   Heavy cream
>   Kirsch

Put in the refrigerator 1 hour before serving 1 cup raspberry or currant jelly, 1 cup cream cheese, the whites of 3 eggs, as well as the bowl from which the dessert is to be served. Five minutes before serving time put the jelly and the cream cheese in the blender at lowest speed. In 1 minute add 2 tablespoons heavy cream and 2 tablespoons of the very best kirsch. In 1 minute more add the whites of 3 eggs. In another minute or two remove from blender to chilled bowl.

Crème Renversée

YOU WILL NEED:
>   Sugar
>   Milk
>   Vanilla bean, caramel, strong coffee, chocolate, kirsch or
>   any preferred liqueur
>   Eggs

This is the classical French dessert.

Put 1 cup sugar over low heat in the mold in which the custard is to be baked. When the sugar is melted turn the mold in all directions so that the sides are completely covered. Remove from heat and put aside. Heat 4 cups of milk with ½ vanilla bean cut in half lengthwise. Break 5 yolks and 7 whites of eggs in a bowl and beat as for an omelette. Slowly pour the sugar and milk over them. Strain into the caramel-covered mold. Put the mold in a pan of hot water and bake slowly in a 200° oven. The water in the pan below should on no account boil. It will take about 40 minutes in the oven. When it is done a silver knife should come out clean. When it does, remove custard from oven and from pan of water. Do not turn out of mold until completely cold.

Crème renversée may be flavored, instead of with vanilla, with 4 tablespoons caramel or 4 tablespoons very strong coffee, or with 3 squares melted chocolate, or with 3 tablespoons kirsch or any preferred liqueur.

It can be served with sauce anglaise (see below).

Sauce Anglaise (or Crème Anglaise)

YOU WILL NEED:
Eggs   Milk
Sugar   Flavoring desired

Stir the yolks of 6 eggs with ¾ cup sugar until pale yellow. Add 2 cups hot milk and place the mixture over very lowest heat, stirring constantly in one direction until the spoon is coated. Remove from heat. Strain and stir frequently until cold.

This sauce may be flavored in any of the ways of the crème renversée.

Praline Powder

YOU WILL NEED:
Sugar
Hazel nuts or almonds or both

Put 1½ cups sugar with ½ cup water in saucepan over medium heat. Stir with wooden spoon until sugar is dissolved, no longer. Pour in at once 2 cups blanched and chopped hazel nuts or almonds or both. (To skin hazel nuts heat in oven with door open and when warm, not toasted, roll in clean cloth.) Cook until syrup becomes golden color. Remove from heat. Pour on lightly oiled plate or table. When cold pound to a powder. Store in covered jar.

Excellent to have on tap for unexpected guests, good for crème anglaise, ices, whipped cream.

Canougats

This mixture will "spin a thread" when it reaches 250° F. It is wise, if you are a beginner, to use a candy thermometer. A word of warning: Never put a cold thermometer directly into boiling liquid. Heat it first in water brought slowly to the boiling point. After using the thermometer place it immediately in very hot water and cool gradually.

YOU WILL NEED:
> *Sugar*
> *Powdered chocolate or cocoa*
> *Light cream*

This is really a bonbon, but is passed in France with the dessert.

Dissolve in double boiler 1 cup sugar with 1 cup powdered chocolate or cocoa in ¼ cup water and 1 cup light cream; cook until it spins a thread. This will take over 20 minutes. Remove from heat and pour into a shallow oiled pan. Cut into squares when cold. Keeps well in covered tin.

CAKES AND COOKIES

Quo Vadis Cake

Miss Toklas' first acceptance of modern cooking gadgets was an electric blender. She was so impressed by it that she sometimes writes her recipes as if they could be achieved by no other method. However, it is quite possible to make this cake in a more orthodox manner by creaming the butter and sugar together and then adding one by one the yolks of the eggs, beating after each addition. The flour in that case is added later bit by bit.

YOU WILL NEED:

> *Sugar*
> *Eggs*
> *Flour*
> *Butter*
> *Crystallized pineapple, cherries, angelica and orange peel*
> *Almonds*

During my mother's frequent absences from home I was often in charge of the household and this was the time when I began to copy recipes into a gray cloth-covered notebook from which I am copying now. This one must have come to my attention after Sienkiewicz's *Quo Vadis?* became a best seller in Europe and then in '96 was translated and published in the United States to become a best seller again. Perhaps my enthusiasm for the kitchen did not long survive the first acquaintance, for there are few entries after this cake. This and several other recipes belong to the same period—pre-Spanish-American War.

Place in blender—it was nearly fifty years later that the blessed blender revolutionized my life—1 cup sugar and the yolks of 6 eggs. When they have doubled in quantity add 1 cup sifted flour and ¼ cup soft butter. When perfectly smooth, remove from blender and fold in ¾ cup finely diced crystallized pineapple, cherries, angelica and orange peel. Then fold in the beaten whites of the 6 eggs. Place in a well-buttered mold that has been sprinkled with slivered almonds. Bake in 325° oven 40 minutes.

Gâteau Gavotte

This is one of the few instances where Miss Toklas recommends refrigeration. She is not enthusiastic about modern mechanical refrigeration. Like many of her French friends she thinks the refrigerator, and especially a mechanical refrigerator, "takes the life out of the food."

Many of Miss Toklas' recipes call for powdered chocolate, which is easy to buy in France but is not generally available in the United States except in combination with sugar as instant chocolate. Cocoa may be used instead but the taste is not quite so rich.

In Paris almond oil would be used to coat the sides of the mold, but since almond oil is difficult to find except perhaps in a pharmacy, peanut oil is an acceptable substitute.

Makes about 1 quart.

YOU WILL NEED:

Milk	Powdered chocolate or cocoa
Sugar	Brandy
Eggs	Peanut oil
Butter	Lady fingers

It was called gâteau gavotte in the collection from which I copied it years ago. It is a dessert, not a cake.

Place 1 cup milk and ½ cup sugar in saucepan over low heat. Stir until sugar is dissolved, slowly add the contents of the saucepan to the well-stirred yolks of 3 eggs. Stir occasionally until cold. Then slowly add to the mixture 1 cup soft butter, ½ cup powdered chocolate or cocoa and 1 tablespoon brandy. Oil a mold with almond or peanut oil and cover the bottom and sides with lady fingers which have been lightly and evenly sprinkled with brandy. Place the cream into the prepared mold. Place in refrigerator for 5 or 6 hours; it can be made the day before but should be removed several hours before serving time. The cream must not be frozen but unctuous.

Queen of Sheba Cake

Miss Toklas suggests flavoring the whipped-cream topping for this dessert cake with ¼ cup "very, very strong cold coffee." A teaspoonful of instant coffee may be used instead.

YOU WILL NEED:
>   *Flour*
>   *Sugar*
>   *Powdered chocolate or cocoa*
>   *Butter*
>   *Eggs*
>   *Cream*
>   *Powdered sugar*
>   *Coffee*

This cake is mixed in an original and easy way, labor- and time-saving.

Mix thoroughly 1 cup sifted flour, 1 cup sugar and ½ cup powdered chocolate or cocoa. Cream ½ cup butter and gradually add the yolks of 4 eggs. Add the dry ingredients to the butter-egg mixture. Beat the whites of the 4 eggs to just the peak point and gently fold in. Bake in a buttered and floured spring form in 300° oven for 40 minutes. Remove from spring form pan when cool. Before serving cover with 1 cup heavy whipped cream to which has been added, while beating, ¼ cup powdered sugar and ¼ cup very, very strong cold coffee.

Lemon Cake

This is an unusual and deliriously delicious if somewhat extrav-agant way to dress up a cake. Splurgy, luscious and lovely, it should provide delight for a dozen diners.

The base, according to Miss Toklas' recipe, is a 6-egg sponge cake. You may use any other type of sponge or sunshine cake or even an angel cake made from a mix.

YOU WILL NEED:
> Eggs   Lemons
> Sugar   Orange

Bake a 6-egg sponge cake. While the cake is cooling in its tin, stir the yolks of 9 eggs with 1 cup sugar until thick and foamy. Then add the juice of 4 lemons and the juice of an orange. Cook in a double boiler until stiff. Then fold in the beaten whites of 9 eggs. Remove cake from tin, place on a piece of foil on cookie sheet and cover with the mixture from the double boiler. Return to 300° oven for 15 minutes.

Cup Cakes

YOU WILL NEED:
> Butter   Baking powder
> Sugar   Milk
> Egg   Vanilla extract
> Pastry flour Flour

Cream ¼ cup butter with ½ cup sugar. Beat 1 egg and add to butter-sugar mixture. Stir well. Sift 1 cup pastry flour. Add 1 teaspoon baking powder and resift. Add to first mixture alter-nately with ¼ cup milk. Add 1 teaspoon vanilla extract and stir until smooth. Pour into buttered and lightly floured muffin tins only half full. Bake in 400° oven 15 to 20 minutes or until golden brown.

These are good frosted.

A Chocolate Glaze

YOU WILL NEED:

    Unsweetened chocolate   Eggs
    Confectioner's sugar   Butter

Melt over hot water 3 squares unsweetened chocolate. When melted remove from heat and add 1½ cups sifted confectioner's sugar and 2½ tablespoons hot water. Add one at a time the yolks of 3 eggs, stirring carefully to incorporate the ingredients. Add one at a time 4 tablespoons butter. Spread on cake. Do not put in refrigerator for it will lose its glaze.

Kerjeans

This is an unusual confection reminiscent of the Near East. Because they are thicker than other cookies, full of fruits and nuts and baked in a coolish oven, the cooking time is rather longer than usual. A powdering of sugar is appropriate.

YOU WILL NEED: Sugar
    Flour   Eggs
    Butter   Ground almonds
    Salt   Crystallized fruits

Mix thoroughly but lightly ½ cup sifted flour, ¼ cup butter, a pinch of salt and ¼ cup sugar. Then add 4 yolks of eggs, ¼ cup ground almonds and 4 tablespoons diced crystallized fruits. When these are well mixed roll out to an inch thickness. Cut out with cookie cutter and bake on buttered baking sheet in a 275° oven about 30 minutes. They should be lightly browned.

Swedish Cookies

This recipe makes about a dozen good-sized cookies. You may want to double or even triple the recipe.

Chopped unblanched almonds or hazel nuts may be used instead of pistachio nuts; crab-apple or guava jelly instead of red currant.

YOU WILL NEED:

Butter	Chopped nuts
Light brown sugar	Red currant jelly
Flour	Chopped pistachio nuts

Cream ½ cup butter, gradually adding ¼ cup sifted light brown sugar and ¼ cup sifted flour. Roll in your hands to balls the size of small walnuts and then roll each ball in chopped nuts. Place on a buttered baking sheet. Flatten the tops. Bake for 5 minutes in a 300° oven. Then remove the sheet from oven and with the handle of a knife make a deep indentation in the center of each cookie. Return the sheet to oven for 15 minutes more baking. Remove with spatula and fill the hollows with red currant jelly and sprinkle some finely chopped pistachios around the edge.

Sablé

In Paris shops you will find packaged sablés but they taste all too much like practically all kinds of packaged cookies and are usually flavored with lemon extract instead of the lightly grated peel of fresh lemons. Made at home they are a real delicacy, rather like Scotch shortbread.

YOU WILL NEED:

	Sugar
Flour	Grated lemon peel
Butter	Eggs

These famous little cakes are named after the small town near the great Benedictine monastery at Solesmes. After Holy Week is over and Easter Mass has been said, everyone precipitates himself upon the excellent baker to buy the "sablés" and to bring them back to Paris.

Mix 2 cups sifted flour, 1 cup butter, 2 cups sugar minus 2

tablespoons, the zest of ½ lemon and the yolks of 2 eggs. Mix well but lightly. Put aside for 2 hours in a cool spot but not in the refrigerator. Then roll out to ⅓-inch thickness, cut with cookie cutter, bake on very lightly buttered baking sheet at 300° for 12 minutes. They must not be colored, just pale butter color.

The next four recipes are of my youth from the gray cloth-covered notebook, in the large angular handwriting affected by girls before the young men they danced with went off to the Spanish-American War.

Brownstone Front

Whether or not Miss Toklas would approve I can't tell, having never discussed the question of frosting mixes. But may I suggest that an excellent "icing" for this or almost any other cake can be made from a packaged frosting mix. The chocolate-rum icing that she prefers is simply made in seconds by substituting rum for the water called for in the package directions.

YOU WILL NEED:

Powdered chocolate or cocoa	*Eggs*
Light brown sugar	*Flour*
Milk	*Baking soda*
Butter	*Vanilla extract*

Not that we knew brownstone fronts in San Francisco. We glimpsed them on our way through New York, on our way to Hoboken to find the boat that was to take us to France.

Cook in double boiler 1 cup powdered chocolate or cocoa, ½ cup light brown sugar and ½ cup milk. When quite smooth remove from heat. Cream ½ cup butter with 1 cup light brown sugar. Add 2 eggs, one at a time, beating well. Combine with chocolate mixture. Sift 2 cups flour with 1 teaspoon baking soda, adding alternately with ½ cup milk. Add 1 tablespoon vanilla extract (we certainly did flavor with extracts in those dark ages). Bake in 2 oblong buttered pans in 300° oven for ½ hour. Turn out to cool on rack. Put together with chocolate icing or rum icing but preferably with chocolate-rum icing.

Prater

Inspired by Vienna, both this cake and its filling may be made with great ease through the use of the electric blender. Instead of adding "¼ cup very, very strong coffee drop by drop" you may simply use a teaspoonful of instant coffee.

YOU WILL NEED:
For the batter:

Eggs	Flour
Sugar	Baking powder
Powdered chocolate or cocoa	Vanilla extract

For the filling:

Butter	Egg yolks
Confectioner's sugar	Coffee

Stir the yolks of 6 eggs with 1 cup sugar until stiff, or, in these days, beat electrically. Sift ¾ cup powdered chocolate or cocoa, ¾ cup flour and ½ teaspoon baking powder. Add to first mixture. Then fold in the beaten whites of 6 eggs and 1 tablespoon vanilla extract. Bake in buttered and floured spring form in 300° oven for ½ hour.

When cold cut in half and horizontally spread with this special Viennese filling: Cream 1 cup butter with 1 cup sifted confectioner's sugar. Slowly add the beaten yolks of 2 eggs and drop by drop ¼ cup very, very strong coffee. If you wish to gild the lily cover with chocolate glaze (see page 135).

Here are two recipes named after two actresses marvelously unlike who graced the stage and thrilled my youth.

I commence politely with the foreigner. It is a very plain cake indeed.

The Ribbons of Sarah Bernhardt

Much more like a pie pastry than a cake or cookie dough, these little ribbons, you will note, contain no sweetening. It is difficult to say just how much milk will be needed. Different types of flour take up different amounts and on different days depending upon the weather and the amount of moisture in the air. You might start with 2 tablespoons, adding more little by little.

Ribbons should be about an inch wide, cut into strips about 3 inches long.

If you like you may sprinkle before baking with vanilla sugar or just plain granulated sugar to make a sweet glisten on top. Makes about 2 dozen.

Very good with a chilled compote of fruit.

YOU WILL NEED:
>Flour
>Butter
>Salt
>Milk

Mix 1 cup flour with ¼ cup butter, a pinch of salt and enough milk to roll quite thin. Cut in ribbons and place on buttered baking sheet. Bake in 375° oven until very lightly colored. Serve hot.

May Irwin's Cake

This might have been a gingerbread except that the pervading flavor is cinnamon instead of ginger and the cake is laden with nuts and raisins.

YOU WILL NEED: *Flour*
      Butter   *Cinnamon*
      Molasses   *Cloves*
      Eggs   *Mixed nuts*
      Soda   *Seedless raisins*

The memory of her blond beauty and throaty throbbing voice: "As I walked the levée round, round, round" has effaced the procession of Loreleis who followed. When I baked this cake the other day it was no surprise to find it as vivid as a portrait of the lustrous lady.

Melt 1 cup butter in ½ cup molasses. Then remove from heat and stir in one at a time the yolks of 3 eggs and 1 teaspoon soda dissolved in a little hot water. Stir in 2¾ cups flour sifted with 1 teaspoon cinnamon and ½ teaspoon cloves. When thoroughly mixed fold in the beaten whites of 3 eggs, 1 pound chopped mixed nuts and ¾ pound chopped seedless raisins. Bake in well-buttered and floured pan in 350° oven for about 35 minutes.

Puff Paste

YOU WILL NEED:
>Flour   Ice water
>Salt   Butter

Mix 2 cups sifted flour and ¼ teaspoon salt on pastry board or marble or enameled top of table. Add little by little some ice water. Work little—you will mix the dough with the tips of the fingers or with a pastry blender until it is as fine as rice. Add enough ice water to be just able to roll into a ball. When it is smooth roll into a ball, cover it and put it aside for several hours. Then roll it out evenly into a square. Place 1 cup kneaded butter at room temperature flattened into a square on the dough and fold the dough over butter to the center from all sides. Turn ¼ to the left and roll out in a long oblong not more than ½ inch thick. Fold over again, turn and roll out again. This is called 2 turns. Put in a covered bowl in refrigerator for ¼ hour. Fold and roll out dough four more times, resting the dough for 15 minutes after each 2 turns. After the 6th turn and its rest of 15 minutes the dough can be rolled out to fit the pie plate or pan, chilling it in refrigerator before baking it in a 400° oven—previously pricking with a fork the bottom of the dough. If you make a covered pie cut a vent in the cover. Pinch the edges prettily together and decorate the top with pastry leaves around the vent.

Half Puff-Paste Dough

Slightly more economical—use ¾ cup butter instead of 1 cup, 2 cups flour, 5 turns instead of 6.

To Make a Puff Paste in 3 Minutes

Mix 1 cup butter with 1 cup minus 3 tablespoons sifted flour, ¼ teaspoon salt and ice water. Give only 4 turns one immediately after the other. Bake at once.

Puff-Paste Dough with Olive Oil

For 2 cups flour take ⅔ cup olive oil. Proceed as above. This dough must be eaten hot.

Puff-Paste Crescents

Follow puff-paste recipe (page 141), and cut with a fluted crescent cookie cutter.

A fluted crescent cookie cutter comes in various sizes. I prefer the medium or small ones.

A Plain Pie-Crust Dough

This crust is rolled twice in the same manner as puff paste. But puff paste gets six turns.

YOU WILL NEED: *Butter*
    Flour   *Salt*

Mix 1 cup and 2 tablespoons sifted flour with ½ cup butter. Knead on board for 10 minutes. Add 3 tablespoons water and a pinch of salt. Put aside for ½ hour. Then give it 2 turns and bake.

Pie Crust Made with Hot Water

YOU WILL NEED: *Flour*
          Butter   *Baking powder*

Pour ¼ cup boiling water over ½ cup butter. Beat with a fork until it becomes a smooth liquid. Sift 1½ cups flour with ⅓ teaspoon baking powder. Sift again into the liquid and stir until even. Chill and roll out. This dough, if well wrapped in foil, keeps well in refrigerator.

ICE CREAMS, PARFAITS

AND SORBETS

Ice Creams

Ice creams are made in various ways, of a variety of flavors, of various ingredients.

The French make them with eggs, sugar and milk or cream and flavoring. The American way is to use the French method but more and more we tend to use cream, heavy cream and whipped cream.

This is the plain way the French prepare a

Vanilla Ice Cream

YOU WILL NEED: Eggs
    Milk   *Sugar*
    Vanilla bean   *Flavorings*

Place 2 cups milk in a saucepan over very low flame with ½ vanilla bean cut in half lengthwise. Stir the yolks of 6 eggs with 1¼ cups sugar until they are pale-yellow-colored. Add the hot milk slowly. Return to heat and stir constantly until the spoon is coated. Remove from heat and stir frequently until cold. Strain and freeze, hand or electric.

To make a plain coffee ice cream the French add 3 tablespoons very strong cold coffee just before freezing.

For a chocolate ice cream they add 3 tablespoons melted chocolate to the hot milk.

For a caramel ice cream they melt ½ cup sugar in a heavy skillet and pour it into the hot milk.

A Richer French Ice Cream

YOU WILL NEED:

> Vanilla-ice-cream mixture (above)
> Heavy cream

Follow their plainer way but add 1 cup heavy cream before freezing.

Praline Ice Cream

YOU WILL NEED:

> Vanilla-ice-cream mixture (above)
> Heavy cream
> Praline powder

To the heavy cream they add 1 cup praline powder (see page 129).

Pistachio Ice Cream

Miss Toklas' method of blanching almonds by letting them stand overnight in cold water is worthy of special notice.

"Everybody knows about the hot-water method," she says, "and everybody has burnt fingers and the nuts by using it. This is a Spanish idea, I think."

Here again the blender may be used instead of the mortar and fine sieve.

YOU WILL NEED:

> Vanilla-ice-cream mixture   Orange-flower water
> Almonds   Green coloring
> Pistachios   Kirsch

Let almonds stand overnight covered with cold water. They will blanch without difficulty. Pound in a mortar ½ cup peeled blanched almonds, ¼ cup peeled pistachios with 1 tablespoon orange-flower water. Pound through a fine sieve. Mix with ice-cream mixture and put aside for 12 hours. Color lightly with green coloring. Add 1 tablespoon kirsch and freeze.

Apricotine Ice Cream

In the United States, crystallized apricots would probably be sold as candied glazed apricots. To emphasize the apricot flavor even more, you might pass a small decanter of apricot brandy or liqueur and let those who wish pour a little over the ice cream.

YOU WILL NEED:
> *Vanilla-ice-cream mixture*
> *Crystallized apricots*
> *Apricot jelly or apricot marmalade*

To a vanilla ice cream (see page 144) add 1 cup diced crystallized apricots. Pour into freezer and pour around the sides 5 or 6 tablespoons apricot jelly or strained apricot marmalade. Freeze. When the ice cream is removed from the mold it will look as if it were apricot tears.

Richelieu Ice Cream

YOU WILL NEED:
> *Vanilla-ice-cream mixture*   *Kirsch*
> *Lady fingers*   *Chocolate sauce*

To a vanilla ice cream just before freezing add 6 lady fingers cut in half lengthwise and soaked in a very little kirsch. Serve with chocolate sauce (see page 123).

Ice Cream of the Hesperides

The golden apples of Hesperides are said by some authorities to have been not apples but oranges. Hence the name of this orange-flavored ice cream.

YOU WILL NEED: *Crystallized orange peel*
    Vanilla-ice-cream mixture   *White curaçao*

To vanilla ice cream add just before freezing 1 cup diced crystallized orange peel and ¼ cup white curaçao.

Chinese Ice Cream

This is one of Alice Toklas' favorite recipes. She esteems it greatly because it has such subtlety. To get green walnuts you should have access to a walnut tree and use the nuts before they ripen.

YOU WILL NEED:
    Green walnuts   *Eggs*
    Honey   *Cream*

Peel and shell ½ pound green walnuts. Break into small pieces. Mix with 1 pound honey. These will give the ice cream its flavor. Stir the yolks of 3 eggs into the mixture. Then fold in the beaten whites of 3 eggs. Freeze until mushy. Beat with electric beater in chilled bowl. Fold in 1 cup chilled whipped cream.

Maraschino Ice Cream

YOU WILL NEED:
    Thin cream   *Powdered sugar*
    Eggs   *Italian maraschino*

Scald 2 cups thin cream. Stir the yolks of 4 eggs until pale yellow, add ½ cup sugar. Pour the scalded cream over them. Beat the whites of 4 eggs, gradually adding ½ cup powdered sugar.

Place the creamy yolks-of-eggs mixture in a double boiler, beat with a whisk. Add the whites of eggs and whisk until the mixture commences to thicken. Remove from heat and stir occasionally until cold. Then add 1 cup veritable Italian maraschino. Freeze.

Do not be misled by the fluid in the bottle of so-called maraschino cherries. It is not.

Monaco Pears

YOU WILL NEED:

Pears	Raspberry jelly
Pistachio ice cream	Kirsch

For 1 quart pistachio ice cream chill 6 table pears in refrigerator for 2 hours, cut in half, remove seeds. When time to serve heap the ice cream into a peak with the aid of a spatula in the center of the dish, place the pears in a border around and pour over the pears a glass of raspberry jelly that has been melted and diluted with 2 tablespoons kirsch.

Pears Helena

YOU WILL NEED:
    Vanilla-ice-cream mixture
    Pears
    Hot chocolate sauce

Freeze 1 quart vanilla ice cream. Serve with lightly poached peeled pears and a hot chocolate sauce (see page 123).

Nelusko Ice Cream

YOU WILL NEED:

Unsweetened chocolate	Eggs
Thin cream	Sugar
	Praline powder

Melt 4 squares chocolate in double boiler with 2 cups thin cream. When quite smooth remove from heat and pour slowly over 6 well-stirred yolks of eggs and 1½ cups sugar. Return to double boiler and stir until spoon is coated. Remove from heat and stir frequently until cold. Add 1 cup praline powder (see page 129) and freeze.

Frozen Biscuit in the Manner of Grand Carême

YOU WILL NEED:

Cup cake	Vanilla ice cream
Strawberry jelly	Strawberry ice cream
Brandy	Heavy cream

Have a rich but light cup cake about 3½ inches high. Cut it in half horizontally with a long sharp knife. With a little strawberry jelly attach one of the layers of cake to the serving dish. Sprinkle on this layer a little good brandy. Place on this layer a 1½-inch layer of vanilla ice cream. Place on this the second layer of cake. On this sprinkle a very little brandy and cover with an inch and a half of strawberry ice cream. Cover the ice cream with heavy sweetened whipped cream. If everything is prepared on the table before you commence to work with the help of a metal spatula you will have no trouble in putting this delicious party dessert together.

Charlotte Glacé à la Princesse

YOU WILL NEED:

	Crystallized fruits
Thin cream	Heavy cream
Sugar	Madeira
Eggs	Lady fingers

Place 2 cups thin cream with 1 cup sugar in a saucepan over low heat. Stir the yolks of 6 eggs until pale lemon colored. Pour over them the scalded cream and sugar. Place over low heat, stirring until spoon is coated. Remove from heat and strain. Stir occasionally until cold. Place in refrigerator tray until half frozen. Dice 1½ cups mixed crystallized fruits. Whip 1 cup heavy cream, gradually adding ⅓ cup good Madeira. Add fruit. Remove mixture from refrigerator and beat with electric beater in chilled bowl. Fold into whipped cream and Madeira. Lightly paint the bottom and sides of charlotte mold with soft sweet butter. Line the mold with lady fingers. Fill with the ice cream and place in freezing compartment of refrigerator for 2 hours. Have ½ cup whipped cream ready to decorate the charlotte when removed from mold ready to serve.

Black-Bread Ice Cream

A popular icebox cake is made with slices of white bread, but the idea of using dark bread in a dinner-party dessert still seems a little startling. You may use whole-wheat bread, rye bread without caraway seeds or even pumpernickel, the Danish or the Jewish kind. Recipe serves at least 8.

YOU WILL NEED: *Sugar*
 Dry brown bread *Thin cream*
 Dry cake   *Heavy cream*
 Eggs   *Brandy*

Crumble 1 cup dry brown bread and 1 cup dry cake. Stir the yolks of 6 eggs and 1 cup sugar until pale yellow. Stir slowly over them 2 cups hot thin cream. Stir over low heat until the spoon is coated. Remove from heat and strain. Stir occasionally until cold. Beat ¾ cup heavy cream and fold with 2 tablespoons brandy into first mixture. Freeze.

A slightly mysterious flavor.

Parfait

Bombes, parfaits, mousses and water ices are made preferably with syrup. A sugar gauge, or syrup gauge, such as Miss Toklas uses can be purchased at the Bazaar Française in New York City.

YOU WILL NEED:
  Syrup
  Eggs
  Cream
  Chocolate, coffee or rum, kirsch or brandy

Parfait is made by stirring 16 yolks of eggs with 2 cups of syrup at 28° sugar gauge over very lowest flame. Stir this mixture until the spoon is coated. Remove from heat, strain and beat over ice until it is absolutely cold. Three-fourths cup of flavoring is then added and 2 cups whipped cream. The flavoring may be chocolate, 4 squares dissolved in thin cream, strong coffee or rum, kirsch or brandy to your taste. Freeze.

Mousse

YOU WILL NEED: *Purée of fruit*
  Syrup   *Cream*

Mousse is made by freezing an equal quantity of syrup (at 35° sugar gauge), of strained purée of fruit, and of whipped cream.

Sorbet, or Water Ice

YOU WILL NEED:
  Fruit juice   *Eggs*
  Sugar syrup   *Sugar*

Sorbet or water ice is made with 2 cups of fruit juice and 2 cups of syrup at 15° sugar gauge and 1 cup of Italian meringue. An Italian meringue is prepared by beating very stiff 2 whites of eggs with ½ cup sugar. Place in double boiler over hot water and beat until it is so stiff that is does not drop from the beater. To this you add the fruit juice and 2 cups syrup. Freeze.

There are many combinations of parfaits, mousses and sorbets. Here are some of them:

Bombe Balmoral

YOU WILL NEED:
>   Sugar   Cream
>   Hazel nuts   Chocolate sauce

Boil 1½ cups sugar with 3 cups water for 5 minutes. Brown lightly in moderate oven 2 cups hazel nuts. Remove from oven. As soon as you can, remove skins by rubbing with a clean cloth. Heat in oven again and when they are hot throw them into boiling syrup. Remove from heat and cover. After 15 minutes remove nuts from syrup and place with ¾ cup water over heat again to extract all the flavor from nuts. Remove nuts and add this water to the syrup and boil slowly for 10 minutes to thicken. When perfectly cold fold in 2 cups whipped cream. Freeze. Serve with chocolate sauce (see page 123).

The nuts may be ground and used on cookies or with icings on cakes.

Water Ice with Champagne

YOU WILL NEED: Muscat grapes
>   Sugar   Bananas
>   Peaches   Kirsch
>   Pears   Champagne

In 1 cup sugar boiled with 2 cups water lightly poach 4 peeled peaches, 4 peeled pears, 1 pound Muscat grapes with skins and seeds removed, and 4 sliced bananas. When the fruit is tender, remove from heat, and reserve liquid. Drain. Soak in 1 cup kirsch for 12 hours, turning occasionally. Prepare a water ice with 2 cups syrup at 12° sugar gauge. Put in tray of refrigerator. When mushy, beat, and fold in 1 pint champagne. Continue to freeze.

Before time to serve reduce syrup the fruits have cooked in and the kirsch they soaked in and pour over them. Serve the water ice on top of the fruit.

A Snowball

YOU WILL NEED:
>   *Vanilla bombe*   *Cream*
>   *Crystallized fruit*   *Liqueur of choice*

Prepare 1 quart vanilla bombe to which has been added 1½ cups diced crystallized fruit. Freeze in a round mold. When it is time to serve, remove from mold to serving dish and thickly cover with 1½ cups of cream whipped with 2 tablespoons of liqueur of your choice.

A Snowball Encrusted with Violets

The same as snowball recipe, adding crystallized violets.

The following are quick, chic and not as suave as the above recipes.

Parfait

YOU WILL NEED:

Eggs   Cream
Sugar   Flavoring

Boil 1 cup of sugar with ¾ cup water until it spins a thread. Pour this syrup over the well-stirred yolks of 3 eggs. When cold fold in the well-beaten whites of 3 eggs. Pour into tray of refrigerator. When mushy remove from tray and beat. Add ¾ cup whipped cream. Return to refrigerator to continue freezing. Can be flavored with any of the flavors for ice cream.

Angel Parfait

YOU WILL NEED:

Sugar   Heavy cream
Eggs   Kirsch

Boil 1 cup sugar with ¾ cup water until it spins a thread. Then pour over the whipped whites of 3 eggs, beating until the mixture is cold. Place in tray of refrigerator. Beat ¾ cup heavy cream with 1 tablespoon kirsch. When contents of tray are mushy beat and fold in the whipped cream. Return to refrigerator to complete freezing.

LIQUEURS AND RATAFIAS

Liqueurs are useful, economical and little trouble to prepare. They are made by soaking in brandy, or more commonly in alcohol, fruits, berries, kernels, skins of citrus fruits and flowers.

Ratafias make delicious flavorings for desserts, in ice creams, parfaits, crème anglaise—what you will or what you have. For butter creams, for puddings, for sauces, in soft drinks and in punches. Combining them is always a pleasure, can become a passion, a pastime.

Vespetro

YOU WILL NEED:

Sugar	Angelica root
Brandy	Powdered orris root
Lemons	Powdered coriander seeds

This is a very old recipe and it has been necessary to consult several dictionaries to know what the exact measurements were and then to translate them into our current American usage. It amused me to find that in the seventeenth century measurements in France differed, those of the capital from those of the provinces. Vespetro is still prepared in the kitchen of a friend of mine. When asked which measurements her cook used she dismissed me with: "Paris, of course."

Place 2 pounds sugar in 2 quarts brandy with 3 sliced lemons, a small piece of angelica root, a pinch of powdered orris root and a pinch of powdered coriander seeds. Cover the jar and infuse for 2 weeks. Then strain, filter and bottle. Cork well.

Vespetro will cure colic, indigestion, vomiting, a stitch in the side (from which at least once during the summer the wives of the farmers at Bilignin suffered), liver complaint, difficulty in urinating, giddiness, rheumatism, difficulty in breathing; and it kills and expels worms from small children (1 teaspoon of Vespetro for 4 or 5 successive mornings). This liqueur will cure those who are in need of help. A man of honor and probity affirms that having been afflicted by an inflammation of the liver from the presence of a gall stone this liqueur caused the expulsion of the stone and his complete cure was achieved in this manner.

Raspberry Ratafia

YOU WILL NEED: *Brandy*
        Raspberries   *Sugar*

As soon as the raspberries began bearing more profusely than we and our guest could consume them, I began making jam and jelly only to find that there were, to our taste, too many seeds. So I betook myself to making ratafia. Once the berries were picked and weighed and the brandy measured—two pounds to three quarts—they were placed in a well-covered jar and there was nothing more to do than to stir the infusion each morning for a month. And to admire the lovely color of the contents of the jar that had to be kept in a light, warm room. The normal summer temperature of our dining room was perfect. At the end of the month strain the contents of the jar and put through a paper filter, bought at a good prescription druggist's. In France this is called a Hippocratus sieve. Boil 2 pounds of sugar in 2 cups of water for 10 minutes. Skim if necessary. When cold add to strained filtered juice and brandy. Bottle and cork tightly.

Strawberries, and currants, black, red or white, make good ratafias in the same way as the raspberries. But better than these there is:

Apricot Ratafia

YOU WILL NEED: *Sugar*
    Apricots   *Brandy*
    White wine   *Stick of cinnamon*

Take 30 sound apricots, cut them in half and remove the pits. Place them in an enameled pot, cover with 4 quarts very good white wine. Place the pot over medium heat. When contents commence to boil add 2 pounds sugar, 1 quart brandy and a 3-inch stick of cinnamon. Remove from heat, cover the pot and allow to infuse for four days. Then strain and filter through a paper. Bottle and cork tightly. Keep in a cool place.

Orange or Mandarin Ratafia

The zest is the outermost part of the peel. The white part is not used, for it gives a bitter taste.

YOU WILL NEED: *Sugar*
    Oranges or mandarins   *Brandy*

Chop the zest of 18 oranges or mandarins. Squeeze the juice of the fruit. Place the zests, juice, 1 pound of sugar and 1 quart brandy into a jar, cover well and infuse for 2 months, shaking it every few days. Strain, filter and bottle. Cork well.

Orange Ratafia

YOU WILL NEED:
    Oranges
    Brandy

This is very good for basting chicken and duck. It gives a fillip if added to a soft drink. Fill a bottle with orange zests, cover them with brandy. Cork well. Shake from time to time. Macerate for 2 months. Strain, filter, bottle and cork well.

Juniper Berry Ratafia

YOU WILL NEED: *Juniper berries*
    Sugar   *Brandy*

Dissolve 2 pounds of sugar in very little hot water and when cold add 2 cups of juniper berries and 1 quart best brandy. Put into jar, cover well and infuse for two weeks, stirring the contents of the jar every 3 days. After 2 weeks strain the contents of the jar and filter through paper. Bottle and cork well. Do not use for several months. Improves with age. This is excellent with roasts and mutton or pork.

Walnut Ratafia

YOU WILL NEED: *Sugar*
    Green walnuts   *Coriander seeds*
    Brandy   *Stick of cinnamon*

Cut in half 20 green walnuts, through which a needle can be pierced. Put into a jar with 1½ quarts brandy. Seal hermetically and infuse in a cool spot for 2 months. Then strain and filter through paper. Take 2 cups of this liquid and pour over 3 pounds of sugar. Add 10 coriander seeds and a 3-inch stick of cinnamon. When the sugar has dissolved bring to the boil. Remove from heat. When cold add to the strained and filtered liquid. Bottle and cork well. Do not use for several months.

This is a stomachic but one needs no such excuse to enjoy it.

Ratafia of Pits

YOU WILL NEED:
> *Apricot or peach pits*
> *Brandy*
> *Sugar*

Half fill a jar with apricot or peach pits or both and cover with brandy. Cover the pot hermetically. Keep in the sun or a warm room for 6 weeks. Then remove ¼ of the pits and crack them with a hammer. Remove the kernels and skin them. Replace the cracked shells and the skinned kernels in the jar. Be sure to cover the jar again. Infuse for 2 weeks more. Then strain through a fine muslin cloth. Then dissolve 1 pound sugar in an equal quantity of water. Add this to the strained liquid. Bottle and cork securely.

Ratafia of Carnations, of Violets or of Orange Blossoms

YOU WILL NEED:
> *Carnations, violets or orange blossoms*
> *Alcohol*
> *Clove*
> *Stick cinnamon*
> *Sugar*

These of course are made separately. Choose your flower or flowers.

Infuse ½ pound of petals, no stamens please, in 1 quart purest grain alcohol with 1 clove and 1 inch of stick cinnamon. Infuse for 1 month. Then strain and filter through paper. Mix with this syrup prepared in advance: 1 pound sugar and 1 cup water which has boiled for 10 minutes. Bottle and cork carefully.

Anise Ratafia

YOU WILL NEED: *Powdered anise*
    Sugar   *Brandy*

Put 1 pound sugar and 1 cup water into a saucepan to boil. Skim and remove from heat when no more scum forms. Then put 1 cup of water over flame. When it is about to boil remove from heat and put into it 1 tablespoon powdered anise. Cover and allow to infuse for ½ hour. Then mix it with the syrup and add 1 quart brandy. Stir well and place in a jar well covered. Keep in sun for 3 weeks. Filter through paper and keep well corked.

Homemade "Maraschino"

Maraschino, literally, is a clear distillate of wild cherries which, of course, this is not. But like true maraschino, it makes an admirable flavoring for fruits, sherbets and all such.

YOU WILL NEED:
    Seville oranges   *Sugar*
    Lemons   *Gin*

Place in a jar the chopped zest of 12 Seville oranges and the chopped zest of 3 lemons. Add 3 pounds sugar and 2 quarts gin. Infuse for 4 days, then strain through a muslin cloth and bottle. Cork tightly.

INDEX

Titles available from
THE COOK'S CLASSIC LIBRARY

AMERICAN TASTE
A Celebration of Gastronomy Coast-to-Coast
JAMES VILLAS
Foreword by James Beard

AROMAS AND FLAVORS OF PAST AND PRESENT
A Book of Exquisite Cooking
ALICE B. TOKLAS
Introduction and Comments by Poppy Cannon

THE ART OF FINE BAKING
PAULA PECK
Introduction by James Beard

HONEY FROM A WEED
Fasting and Feasting in Tuscany, Catalonia, the Cyclades and Apulia
PATIENCE GRAY
Foreword by John Thorne

MICHAEL FIELD'S COOKING SCHOOL
MICHAEL FIELD
Foreword by James Villas

THE MUSHROOM FEAST
A Celebration of Edible Fungi With Over 250 Recipes
JANE GRIGSON
Foreword by Betty Fussell

AN OMELETTE AND A GLASS OF WINE
ELIZABETH DAVID
Foreword by John Thorne

SIX THOUSAND YEARS OF BREAD
Its Holy and Unholy History
H. E. JACOB
Introduction by Lynn Alley

THE UNPREJUDICED PALATE
Classic Thoughts on Food and the Good Life
ANGELO PELLEGRINI
Afterword by M. F. K. Fisher

The Lyons Press
31 West 21 Street · New York, New York 10010
(tel) 212/620-9580 · (fax) 212/929-1836